Windows® 2000 Professional Simplified™

IDG's 3-D Visual™ Series

IDG BOOKS

From
maranGraphics™

IDG Books Worldwide, Inc.
An International Data Group Company
Foster City, CA • Indianapolis • Chicago • New York

Windows® 2000 Professional Simplified™

Published by
IDG Books Worldwide, Inc.
An International Data Group Company
919 E. Hillsdale Blvd., Suite 400
Foster City, CA 94404
(650) 655-3000

Copyright© 1999 by maranGraphics Inc.
     5755 Coopers Avenue
     Mississauga, Ontario, Canada
     L4Z 1R9

Library of Congress Catalog Card No.: 99-068239
ISBN: 0-7645-3422-X
Printed in the United States of America
10 9 8 7 6 5 4 3 2

Distributed in the United States by IDG Books Worldwide, Inc.
Distributed by CDG Books Canada Inc. for Canada; by Transworld Publishers Limited in the United Kingdom; by IDG Norge Books for Norway; by IDG Sweden Books for Sweden; by IDG Books Australia Publishing Corporation Pty. Ltd. for Australia and New Zealand; by TransQuest Publishers Pte Ltd. for Singapore, Malaysia, Thailand, Indonesia, and Hong Kong; by Gotop Information Inc. for Taiwan; by ICG Muse, Inc. for Japan; by Intersoft for South Africa; by Eyrolles for France; by International Thomson Publishing for Germany, Austria and Switzerland; by Distribuidora Cuspide for Argentina; by LR International for Brazil; by Galileo Libros for Chile; by Ediciones ZETA S.C.R. Ltda. for Peru; by WS Computer Publishing Corporation, Inc. for the Philippines; by Contemporanea de Ediciones for Venezuela; by Express Computer Distributors for the Caribbean and West Indies; by Micronesia Media Distributor, Inc. for Micronesia; by Chips Computadoras S.A. de C.V. for Mexico; by Editorial Norma de Panama S.A. for Panama; by American Bookshops for Finland.
For corporate orders, please call maranGraphics at 800-469-6616.
For general information on IDG Books Worldwide's books in the U.S., please call our Consumer Customer Service department at 800-762-2974.
For reseller information, including discounts and premium sales, please call our Reseller Customer Service department at 800-434-3422.
For information on where to purchase IDG Books Worldwide's books outside the U.S., please contact our International Sales department at 317-596-5530 or fax 317-596-5692.
For consumer information on foreign language translations, please contact our Customer Service department at 1-800-434-3422, fax 317-596-5692, or e-mail rights@idgbooks.com.
For information on licensing foreign or domestic rights, please phone 1-650-655-3109.
For sales inquiries and special prices for bulk quantities, please contact our Sales department at 650-655-3200.
For information on using IDG Books Worldwide's books in the classroom or for ordering examination copies, please contact our Educational Sales department at 800-434-2086 or fax 317-596-5499.
For press review copies, author interviews, or other publicity information, please contact our Public Relations department at 650-655-3000 or fax 650-655-3299.
For authorization to photocopy items for corporate, personal, or educational use, please contact maranGraphics at 800-469-6616.
Screen shots displayed in this book are based on pre-release software and are subject to change.

Trademark Acknowledgments

Permissions

©1999 maranGraphics, Inc.

The 3-D illustrations are the copyright of maranGraphics, Inc.

U.S. Corporate Sales	**U.S. Trade Sales**
Contact maranGraphics at (800) 469-6616 or fax (905) 890-9434.	Contact IDG Books at (800) 434-3422 or (650) 655-3000.

ABOUT IDG BOOKS WORLDWIDE

Welcome to the world of IDG Books Worldwide.

IDG Books Worldwide, Inc., is a subsidiary of International Data Group, the world's largest publisher of computer-related information and the leading global provider of information services on information technology. IDG was founded more than 30 years ago by Patrick J. McGovern and now employs more than 9,000 people worldwide. IDG publishes more than 290 computer publications in over 75 countries. More than 90 million people read one or more IDG publications each month.

Launched in 1990, IDG Books Worldwide is today the #1 publisher of best-selling computer books in the United States. We are proud to have received eight awards from the Computer Press Association in recognition of editorial excellence and three from Computer Currents' First Annual Readers' Choice Awards. Our best-selling ...*For Dummies*® series has more than 50 million copies in print with translations in 31 languages. IDG Books Worldwide, through a joint venture with IDG's Hi-Tech Beijing, became the first U.S. publisher to publish a computer book in the People's Republic of China. In record time, IDG Books Worldwide has become the first choice for millions of readers around the world who want to learn how to better manage their businesses.

Our mission is simple: Every one of our books is designed to bring extra value and skill-building instructions to the reader. Our books are written by experts who understand and care about our readers. The knowledge base of our editorial staff comes from years of experience in publishing, education, and journalism — experience we use to produce books to carry us into the new millennium. In short, we care about books, so we attract the best people. We devote special attention to details such as audience, interior design, use of icons, and illustrations. And because we use an efficient process of authoring, editing, and desktop publishing our books electronically, we can spend more time ensuring superior content and less time on the technicalities of making books.

You can count on our commitment to deliver high-quality books at competitive prices on topics you want to read about. At IDG Books Worldwide, we continue in the IDG tradition of delivering quality for more than 30 years. You'll find no better book on a subject than one from IDG Books Worldwide.

John Kilcullen
Chairman and CEO
IDG Books Worldwide, Inc.

Steven Berkowitz
President and Publisher
IDG Books Worldwide, Inc.

Eighth Annual Computer Press Awards ≥1992

Ninth Annual Computer Press Awards ≥1993

Tenth Annual Computer Press Awards ≥1994

Eleventh Annual Computer Press Awards ≥1995

IDG is the world's leading IT media, research and exposition company. Founded in 1964, IDG had 1997 revenues of $2.05 billion and has more than 9,000 employees worldwide. IDG offers the widest range of media options that reach IT buyers in 75 countries representing 95% of worldwide IT spending. IDG's diverse product and services portfolio spans six key areas including print publishing, online publishing, expositions and conferences, market research, education and training, and global marketing services. More than 90 million people read one or more of IDG's 290 magazines and newspapers, including IDG's leading global brands — Computerworld, PC World, Network World, Macworld and the Channel World family of publications. IDG Books Worldwide is one of the fastest-growing computer book publishers in the world, with more than 700 titles in 36 languages. The "...For Dummies®" series alone has more than 50 million copies in print. IDG offers online users the largest network of technology-specific Web sites around the world through IDG.net (http://www.idg.net), which comprises more than 225 targeted Web sites in 55 countries worldwide. International Data Corporation (IDC) is the world's largest provider of information technology data, analysis and consulting, with research centers in over 41 countries and more than 400 research analysts worldwide. IDG World Expo is a leading producer of more than 168 globally branded conferences and expositions in 35 countries including E3 (Electronic Entertainment Expo), Macworld Expo, ComNet, Windows World Expo, ICE (Internet Commerce Expo), Agenda, DEMO, and Spotlight. IDG's training subsidiary, ExecuTrain, is the world's largest computer training company, with more than 230 locations worldwide and 785 training courses. IDG Marketing Services helps industry-leading IT companies build international brand recognition by developing global integrated marketing programs via IDG's print, online and exposition products worldwide. Further information about the company can be found at www.idg.com.   1/24/99

maranGraphics is a family-run business located near Toronto, Canada.

At **maranGraphics**, we believe in producing great computer books–one book at a time.

Each maranGraphics book uses the award-winning communication process that we have been developing over the last 25 years. Using this process, we organize screen shots, text and illustrations in a way that makes it easy for you to learn new concepts and tasks.

We spend hours deciding the best way to perform each task, so you don't have to! Our clear, easy-to-follow screen shots and instructions walk you through each task from beginning to end.

Our detailed illustrations go hand-in-hand with the text to help reinforce the information. Each illustration is a labor of love–some take up to a week to draw!

We want to thank you for purchasing what we feel are the best computer books money can buy. We hope you enjoy using this book as much as we enjoyed creating it!

Sincerely,

The Maran Family

Please visit us on the Web at:
www.maran.com

Credits

Authors:
Kelleigh Wing
Ruth Maran

Technical Consultants:
Paul Whitehead
Eric Kramer

Project Manager:
Judy Maran

Editors:
Raquel Scott
Janice Boyer
Stacey Morrison

Screen Captures:
James Menzies

Layout Designer:
Treena Lees

Illustrators:
Russ Marini
Jamie Bell
Peter Grecco
Sean Johannesen
Steven Schaerer

Screen Artist & Illustrator:
Jimmy Tam

Indexer:
Raquel Scott

Permissions Coordinator:
Jenn Reid

Post Production:
Robert Maran

**Senior Vice President,
Technology Publishing
IDG Books Worldwide:**
Richard Swadley

**Editorial Support
IDG Books Worldwide:**
Barry Pruett
Martine Edwards

Acknowledgments

Thanks to the dedicated staff of maranGraphics, including
Jamie Bell, Cathy Benn, Janice Boyer, Peter Grecco,
Sean Johannesen, Eric Kramer, Wanda Lawrie, Frances Lea,
Treena Lees, Jill Maran, Judy Maran, Robert Maran,
Sherry Maran, Russ Marini, James Menzies, Stacey Morrison,
Jenn Reid, Steven Schaerer, Raquel Scott, Jimmy Tam,
Roxanne Van Damme and Paul Whitehead.

Finally, to Richard Maran who originated the easy-to-use
graphic format of this guide. Thank you for your
inspiration and guidance.

Table of Contents

CHAPTER 1

WINDOWS BASICS

CHAPTER 2

CREATE DOCUMENTS

Trafalgar High School celebra
anniversary this year! We will
on September 10th with an Oper
followed by a buffet dinner.

CHAPTER 3

CREATE PICTURES

CHAPTER 4

VIEW FILES

CHAPTER 5

WORK WITH FILES

Table of Contents

CHAPTER 10

WORK ON A NETWORK

CHAPTER 11

BROWSE THE WEB

CHAPTER 12

EXCHANGE ELECTRONIC MAIL

Microsoft® Windows® 2000 is a program that controls the overall activity of your computer.

Windows ensures that all parts of your computer work together smoothly and efficiently.

WORK WITH FILES

Windows provides ways to organize and manage the files stored on your computer. You can open, sort, rename, move, print, find and delete files.

Windows includes a word processing program, called WordPad, and a drawing program, called Paint, to help you quickly start creating files.

CUSTOMIZE WINDOWS

You can customize Windows in many ways. You can add a colorful design to your screen, change the way your mouse works and change the amount of information that fits on the screen.

OPTIMIZE YOUR COMPUTER

Windows provides tools to help you optimize your computer. You can check your hard disk for errors, remove unnecessary files and defragment your hard disk to improve its performance.

HAVE FUN WITH WINDOWS

You can use Windows to play games, listen to music CDs and assign sounds to program events.

WORK ON A NETWORK

Windows allows you to share equipment and information on a network. You can specify exactly who you want to have access to your printer and each folder on your computer by assigning permissions.

BROWSE THE WEB

Windows lets you browse through the vast amount of information on the World Wide Web. You can move between Web pages you have viewed, create a list of favorite Web pages and search for Web pages of interest.

EXCHANGE E-MAIL AND FAXES

Windows allows you to exchange electronic mail with people around the world. You can reply to, forward and print e-mail messages. Windows also includes a program that allows you to send and receive faxes using your computer's modem.

PARTS OF THE WINDOWS 2000 SCREEN

> The Windows screen displays various items. The items that appear depend on how your computer is set up.

My Documents

Provides a convenient place to store your documents.

My Computer

Lets you view all the folders and files stored on your computer.

My Network Places

Lets you view all the folders and files available on your network.

Recycle Bin

Stores deleted files and allows you to recover them later.

Start Button

Gives you quick access to programs, files and Windows Help.

Quick Launch Toolbar

Gives you quick access to commonly used features, including the desktop, Internet Explorer and Outlook Express.

Taskbar

Displays a button for each open window on your screen. You can use these buttons to switch between open windows.

Title Bar

Displays the name of an open window.

Window

A rectangle on your screen that displays information.

Desktop

The background area of your screen.

A mouse is a handheld device that lets you select and move items on your screen.

When you move the mouse on your desk, the mouse pointer on your screen moves in the same direction. The mouse pointer assumes different shapes, such as ⇖ or I, depending on its location on your screen and the task you are performing.

Resting your hand on the mouse, use your thumb and two rightmost fingers to move the mouse on your desk. Use your two remaining fingers to press the mouse buttons.

MOUSE ACTIONS

Click

Press and release the left mouse button.

Double-click

Quickly press and release the left mouse button twice.

Right-click

Press and release the right mouse button.

Drag

Position the mouse pointer over an object on your screen and then press and hold down the left mouse button. Still holding down the button, move the mouse to where you want to place the object and then release the button.

START WINDOWS

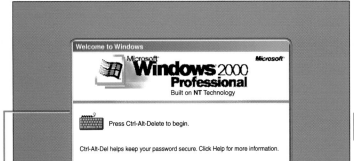

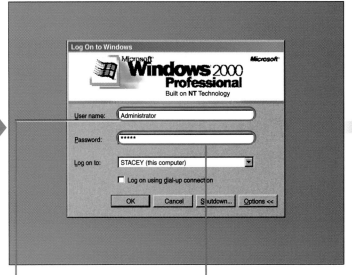

1 Turn on your computer and monitor.

■ The Welcome to Windows dialog box appears.

2 To log on to Windows, press and hold down the `Ctrl` and `Alt` keys as you press the `Delete` key.

■ The Log On to Windows dialog box appears.

■ This area displays your user name.

Note: To enter a different user name, drag the mouse I over the current name until the text is highlighted. Then type a new name.

3 Click this area and then type your password. An asterisk (*) appears for each character you type to prevent others from seeing your password.

What is a domain?

A domain is a group of computers on a network that are administered together. When logging on to Windows, you can log on to a domain on the network or your own computer. If you are not connected to a network, you will not be able to log on to a domain.

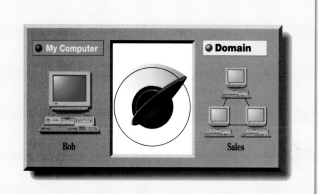

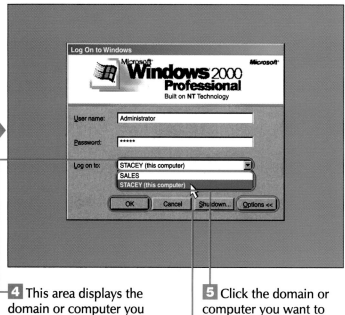

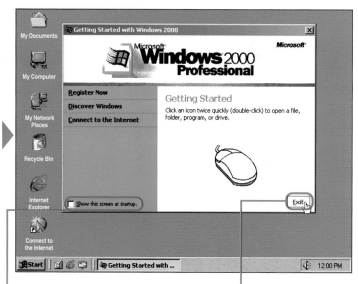

4 This area displays the domain or computer you will log on to. To select a different domain or computer, click this area.

5 Click the domain or computer you want to log on to.

■ If the area is not displayed, click **Options**.

6 Click **OK**.

■ The Getting Started with Windows 2000 dialog box appears.

7 If you do not want this dialog box to appear each time you start Windows, click this option (☑ changes to ☐).

8 Click **Exit** to close the dialog box.

You can use the Start button to start your programs.

START A PROGRAM

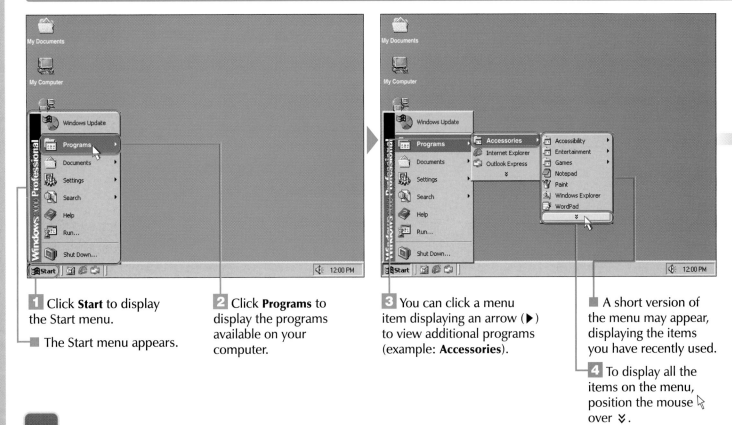

1 Click **Start** to display the Start menu.

■ The Start menu appears.

2 Click **Programs** to display the programs available on your computer.

3 You can click a menu item displaying an arrow (▶) to view additional programs (example: **Accessories**).

■ A short version of the menu may appear, displaying the items you have recently used.

4 To display all the items on the menu, position the mouse over ≫.

Which programs does Windows provide?

Windows comes with many useful programs.

WordPad is a word processing program that lets you create letters, reports and memos.

Paint is a drawing program that lets you draw pictures and maps.

CD Player is a program that lets you play music CDs while you work.

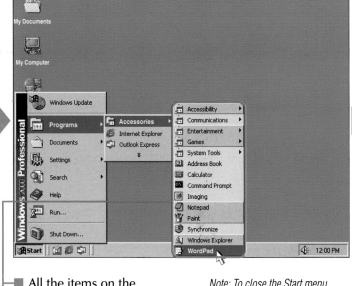

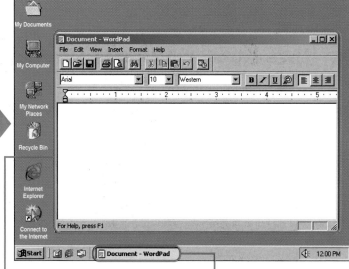

■ All the items on the menu appear.

5 Click the program you want to start (example: **WordPad**).

Note: To close the Start menu without selecting a program, click outside the menu area or press the **Alt** *key.*

■ In this example, the WordPad window appears.

■ A button for the open window appears on the taskbar.

You can enlarge a window to fill your screen. This lets you view more of the window's contents.

MAXIMIZE A WINDOW

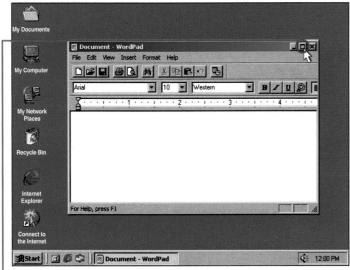

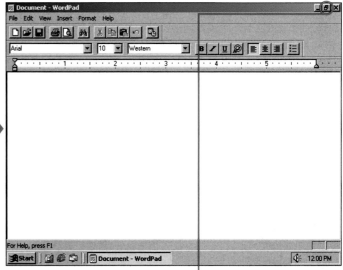

1 Click 🗖 in the window you want to maximize.

■ The window fills your screen.

■ To return the window to its previous size, click 🗗 .

10

MINIMIZE A WINDOW

If you are not using a window, you can minimize the window to remove it from your screen. You can redisplay the window at any time.

MINIMIZE A WINDOW

1 Click ◘ in the window you want to minimize.

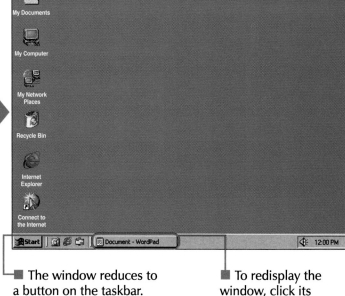

■ The window reduces to a button on the taskbar.

■ To redisplay the window, click its button on the taskbar.

If a window covers items on your screen, you can move the window to a different location.

MOVE A WINDOW

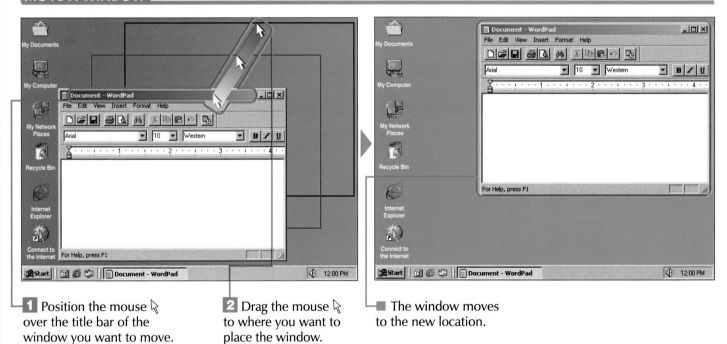

1 Position the mouse ⍚ over the title bar of the window you want to move.

2 Drag the mouse ⍚ to where you want to place the window.

■ The window moves to the new location.

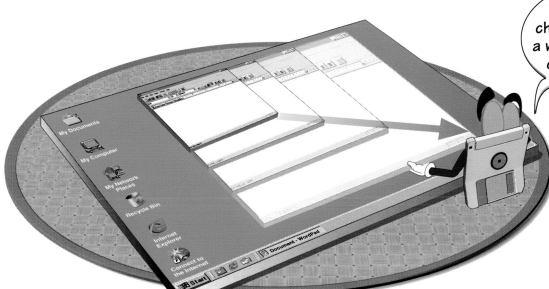

You can easily change the size of a window displayed on your screen.

Enlarging a window lets you view more of its contents. Reducing a window lets you view items covered by the window.

SIZE A WINDOW

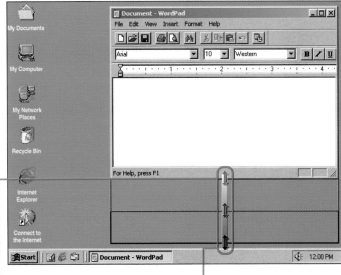

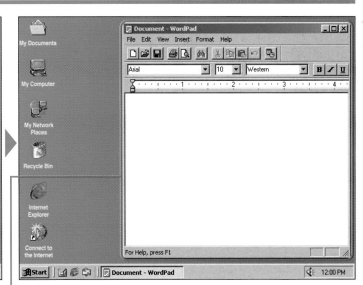

1 Position the mouse ⌖ over an edge of the window you want to size (⌖ changes to ↕, ↔ or ↘).

2 Drag the mouse ↕ until the window displays the size you want.

■ The window displays the new size.

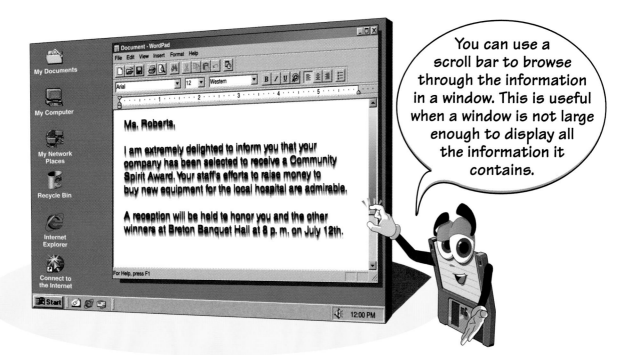

You can use a scroll bar to browse through the information in a window. This is useful when a window is not large enough to display all the information it contains.

SCROLL DOWN

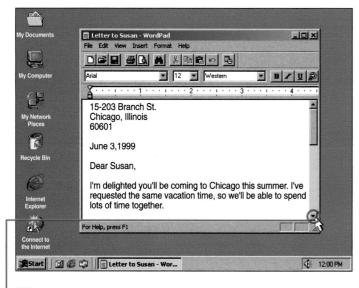

1 Click ▼ to scroll down through the information in a window.

SCROLL UP

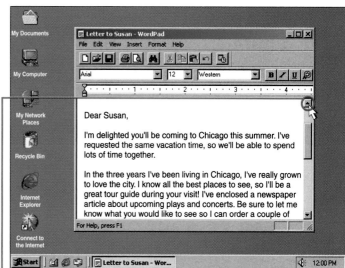

1 Click ▲ to scroll up through the information in a window.

Is there another way to use a mouse to scroll through a window?

You can purchase a mouse with a wheel between the left and right mouse buttons. Moving this wheel lets you scroll through a window.

SCROLL TO ANY POSITION

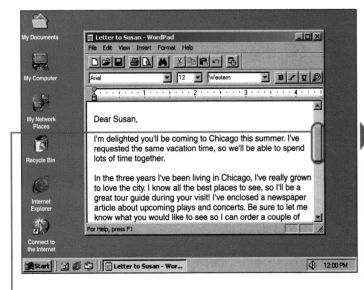

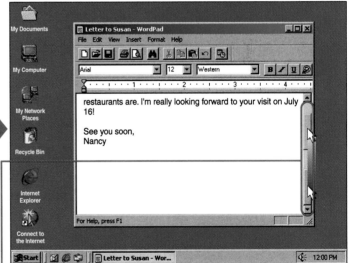

■ The location of the scroll box indicates which part of the window you are viewing. For example, when the scroll box is halfway down the scroll bar, you are viewing information from the middle of the window.

Note: The size of the scroll box varies, depending on the amount of information the window contains and the size of the window.

1 Drag the scroll box along the scroll bar until the information you want to view appears.

You can have more than one window open at a time. You can easily switch between all the windows you have open.

Each window is like a separate piece of paper. Switching between windows lets you place a different piece of paper at the top of the pile.

SWITCH BETWEEN WINDOWS

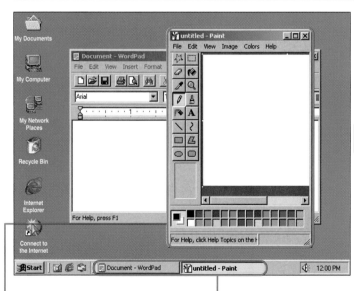

■ You can work in only one window at a time. The active window (example: Paint) appears in front of all other windows and displays a blue title bar.

■ The taskbar displays a button for each open window.

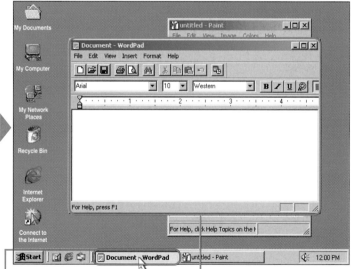

1 To display the window you want to work with in front of all other windows, click its button on the taskbar.

■ The window appears in front of all other windows. This lets you clearly view the contents of the window.

When you finish working with a window, you can close the window to remove it from your screen.

CLOSE A WINDOW

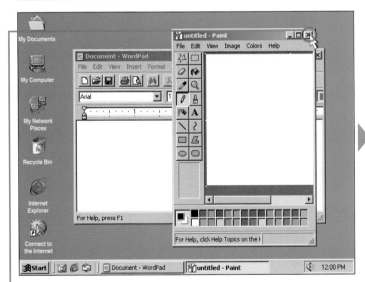

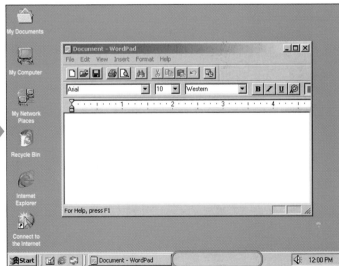

1 Click ✕ in the window you want to close.

■ The window disappears from your screen.

■ The button for the window disappears from the taskbar.

You can instantly minimize all your open windows to remove them from your screen. This allows you to clearly view the desktop.

SHOW THE DESKTOP

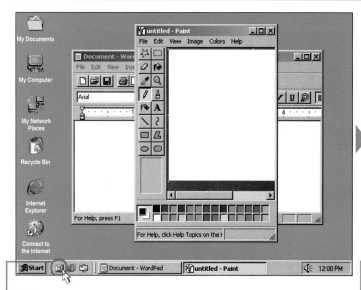

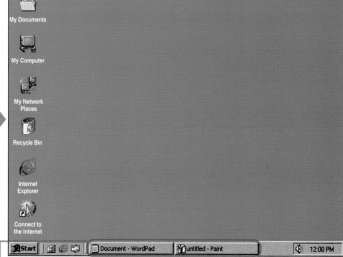

1 Click  to minimize all the open windows on your screen.

■ Each window minimizes to a button on the taskbar. You can now clearly view the desktop.

■ To redisplay a window, click its button on the taskbar.

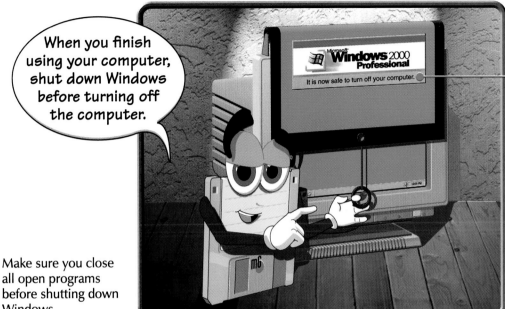

When you finish using your computer, shut down Windows before turning off the computer.

■ Do not turn off your computer until this message appears on your screen.

Make sure you close all open programs before shutting down Windows.

SHUT DOWN WINDOWS

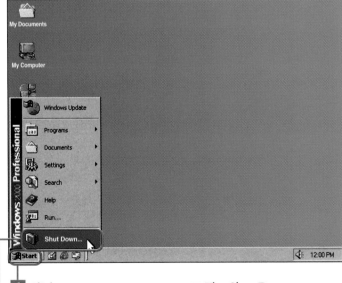

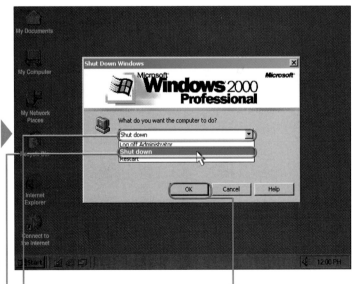

1 Click **Start**.

2 Click **Shut Down**.

■ The Shut Down Windows dialog box appears.

3 To specify that you want to shut down Windows, click this area.

4 Click **Shut down**.

5 Click **OK** to shut down your computer.

If you share your computer with others, you can log off so another person can log on and use the computer.

Make sure you save your information and close your programs before logging off.

LOG OFF YOUR COMPUTER

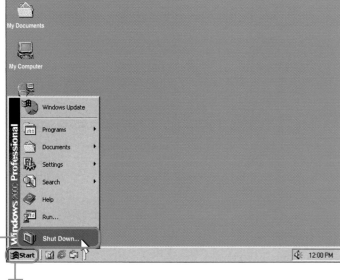

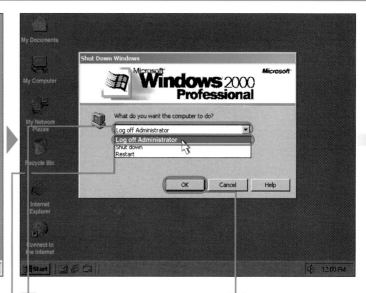

1 Click **Start**.

2 Click **Shut Down**.

■ The Shut Down Windows dialog box appears.

3 To specify that you want to log off Windows, click this area.

4 Click **Log off**.

5 Click **OK** to log off your computer.

Why do I need to enter a user name and password each time I log on to a computer or network?

The user name and password you enter determines the type of access you will have on the computer or network. For example, if you log on as a user, you may not have permission to perform some tasks, such as installing hardware. If you log on as an administrator, you will have permission to perform any task.

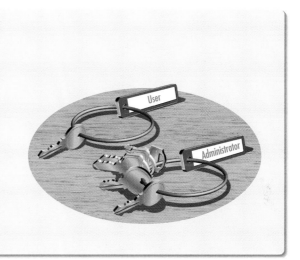

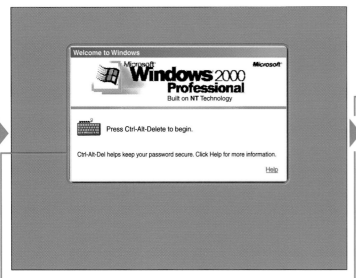

■ The Welcome to Windows dialog box appears.

6 To log on as a different user, press and hold down the Ctrl and Alt keys as you press the Delete key.

■ The Log On to Windows dialog box appears.

7 To enter a different user name, drag the mouse I over the current name until the text is highlighted. Then type a new name.

8 Click this area and then type the password.

9 Click **OK** to log on to the network.

If you are leaving your desk for a short period of time, you can lock your computer so other people cannot access your information.

LOCK YOUR COMPUTER

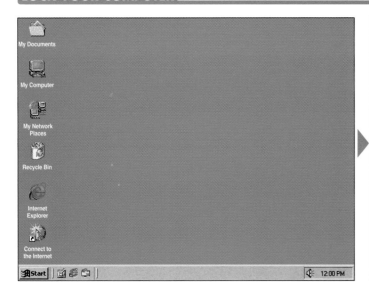

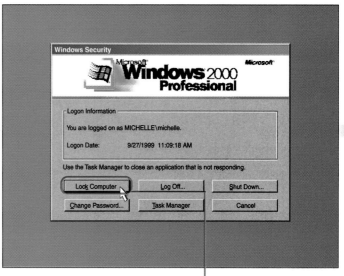

1 Press and hold down the Ctrl and Alt keys as you press the Delete key.

■ The Windows Security dialog box appears.

2 Click **Lock Computer**.

22

Can I hide my information without locking my computer?

Yes. You can turn off your monitor or set up a screen saver to hide the contents of your screen. Hiding the contents of your screen will not prevent others from accessing information on your computer. To set up a screen saver, see page 98.

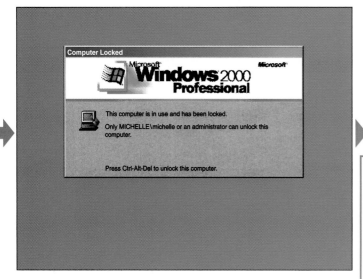

■ The Computer Locked dialog box appears.

3 When you return to your desk and want to unlock the computer, press and hold down the `Ctrl` and `Alt` keys as you press the `Delete` key.

■ The Unlock Computer dialog box appears.

■ This area displays your user name.

4 Type your password. An asterisk (*) appears for each character you type to prevent others from seeing your password.

5 Click **OK**.

If you do not know how to perform a task, you can use the Help feature to get information.

HELP DESK

GETTING HELP

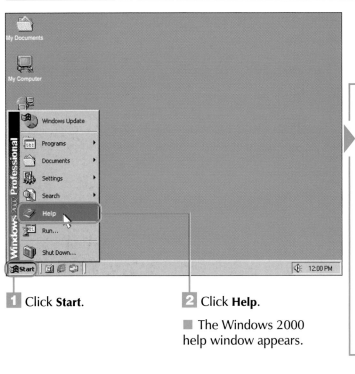

1 Click **Start**.

2 Click **Help**.

■ The Windows 2000 help window appears.

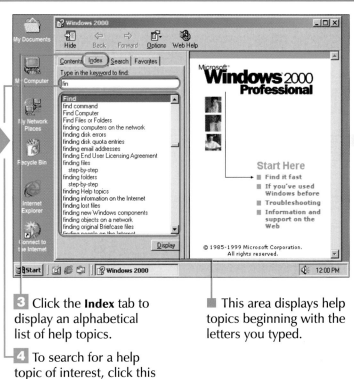

3 Click the **Index** tab to display an alphabetical list of help topics.

4 To search for a help topic of interest, click this area and then type the first few letters of the topic.

■ This area displays help topics beginning with the letters you typed.

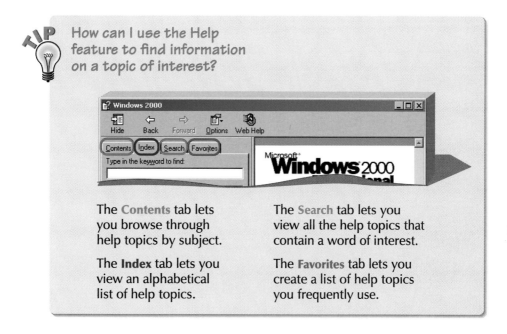

How can I use the Help feature to find information on a topic of interest?

The **Contents** tab lets you browse through help topics by subject.

The **Index** tab lets you view an alphabetical list of help topics.

The **Search** tab lets you view all the help topics that contain a word of interest.

The **Favorites** tab lets you create a list of help topics you frequently use.

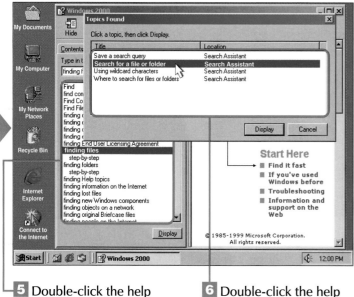

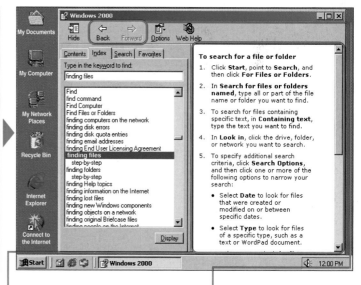

5 Double-click the help topic you want to display information on.

■ The Topics Found dialog box may appear, displaying a list of related help topics.

6 Double-click the help topic of interest.

■ The information on the help topic appears in this area.

■ You can click **Back** or **Forward** to move through the help topics you have viewed.

CHAPTER 2

CREATE DOCUMENTS

Are you interested in creating documents, such as letters and memos? This chapter will show you how to use the WordPad program.

Dear Kevin:

ol celebrates its 30th
We will be celebrating
h an Open House,

WordPad allows you to create simple documents, such as letters and memos.

START WORDPAD

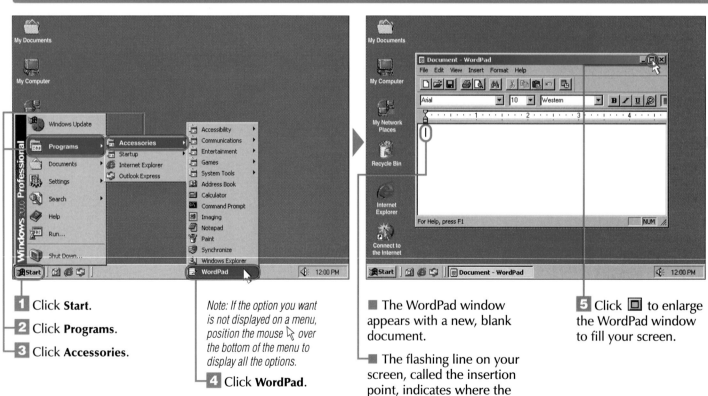

1 Click **Start**.

2 Click **Programs**.

3 Click **Accessories**.

Note: If the option you want is not displayed on a menu, position the mouse ⌖ over the bottom of the menu to display all the options.

4 Click **WordPad**.

■ The WordPad window appears with a new, blank document.

■ The flashing line on your screen, called the insertion point, indicates where the text you type will appear.

5 Click ▢ to enlarge the WordPad window to fill your screen.

Does WordPad offer all the
features I need?

WordPad is a simple program that
offers only basic word processing
features. If you need more advanced
features, you can purchase a more
powerful word processor, such as
Microsoft Word or Corel WordPerfect.
These programs include features,
such as tables, graphics, a spell
checker and a thesaurus.

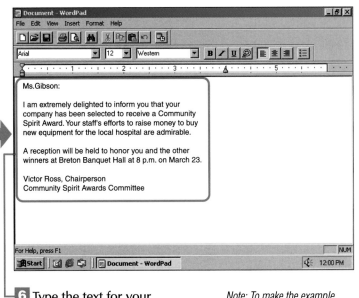

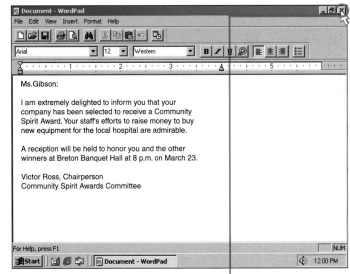

6 Type the text for your
document.

■ When you reach the end of
a line, WordPad automatically
moves the text to the next
line. You need to press the
Enter key only when you
want to start a new line or
paragraph.

*Note: To make the example
easier to read, the font size
has been changed. To change
the font size, see page 37.*

**When you finish using
WordPad, you can exit the
program.**

1 Before exiting WordPad,
save any changes you made
to the document. To save
your changes, see page 32.

2 Click ☒ to exit
WordPad.

You can easily add new text to your document and remove text you no longer need.

INSERT TEXT

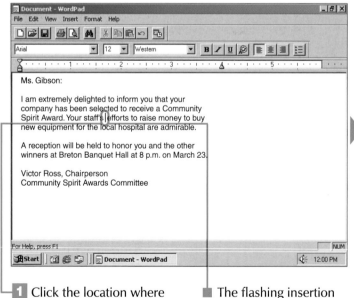

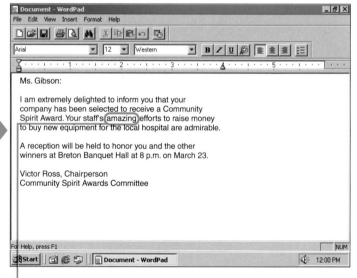

1 Click the location where you want to insert text.

■ The flashing insertion point indicates where the text you type will appear.

2 Type the text you want to insert.

3 To insert a blank space, press the **Spacebar**.

Note: The words to the right of the new text move forward.

How do I cancel changes I made?

WordPad remembers the last changes you made to your document. If you regret a change, you can cancel the change by using the Undo feature.

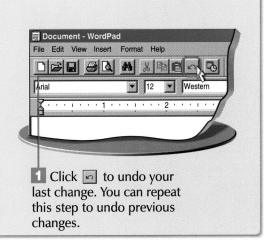

1 Click 🔄 to undo your last change. You can repeat this step to undo previous changes.

DELETE TEXT

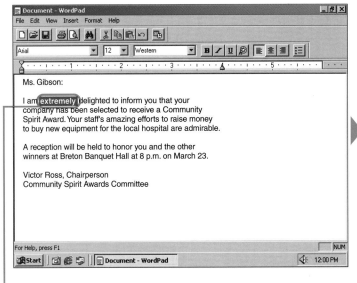

1 To select the text you want to delete, drag the mouse ⌶ over the text until the text is highlighted.

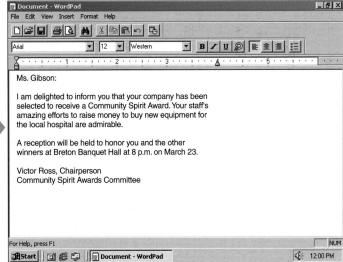

2 Press the Delete key to remove the text.

■ To delete one character at a time, click to the left of the first character you want to delete. Press the Delete key for each character you want to remove.

You should save your document to store it for future use. This lets you later retrieve the document for reviewing or editing.

You should regularly save changes you make to a document to avoid losing your work.

SAVE A DOCUMENT

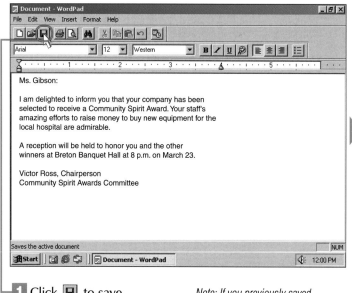

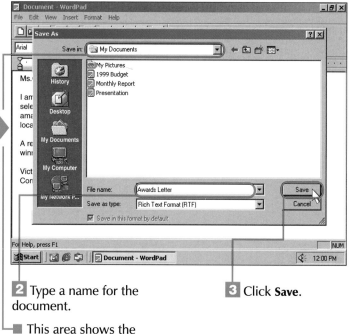

1 Click 💾 to save the document.

■ The Save As dialog box appears.

Note: If you previously saved the document, the Save As dialog box will not appear since you have already named the document.

2 Type a name for the document.

■ This area shows the location where WordPad will store the document. You can click this area to change the location.

3 Click **Save**.

You can produce a paper copy of the document displayed on your screen.

PRINT A DOCUMENT

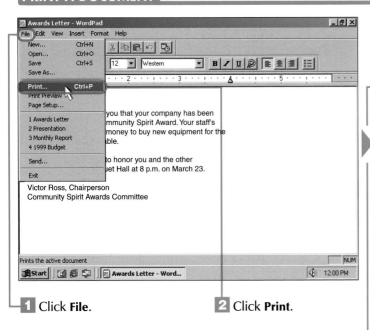

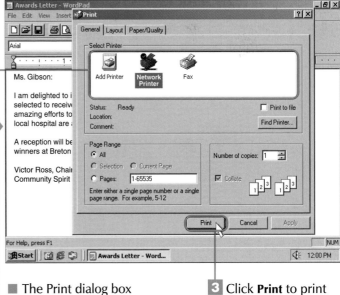

1 Click **File**.

2 Click **Print**.

■ The Print dialog box appears.

■ This area displays the available printers. The printer that will print the document displays a check mark (✔).

3 Click **Print** to print the document.

You can open a saved document and display the document on your screen. This allows you to view and make changes to the document.

OPEN A DOCUMENT

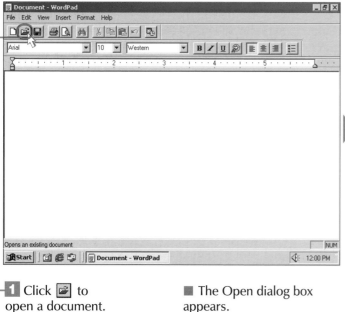

1 Click 📂 to open a document.

■ The Open dialog box appears.

■ This area shows the location of the displayed documents. You can click this area to change the location.

2 Click the name of the document you want to open.

Note: If you cannot find the document you want to open, see page 86.

3 Click **Open**.

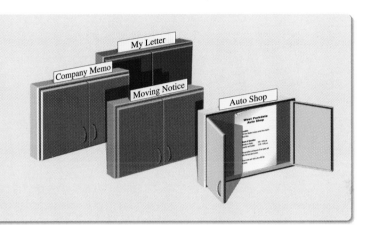

 Can I work with two WordPad
documents at the same time?

WordPad lets you work with only
one document at a time. If you are
currently working with a document,
save the document before opening
another. For information on saving
a document, see page 32.

QUICKLY OPEN A DOCUMENT

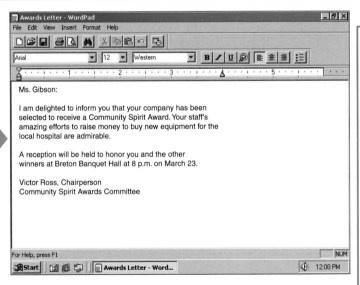

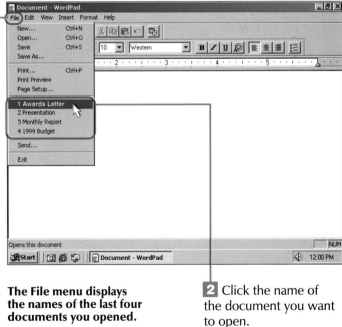

■ WordPad opens the
document and displays
it on your screen. You
can now review and make
changes to the document.

**The File menu displays
the names of the last four
documents you opened.**

1 To quickly open a
document, click **File**.

2 Click the name of
the document you want
to open.

CHANGE FONT TYPE

You can enhance the appearance of your document by changing the design of the text.

CHANGE FONT TYPE

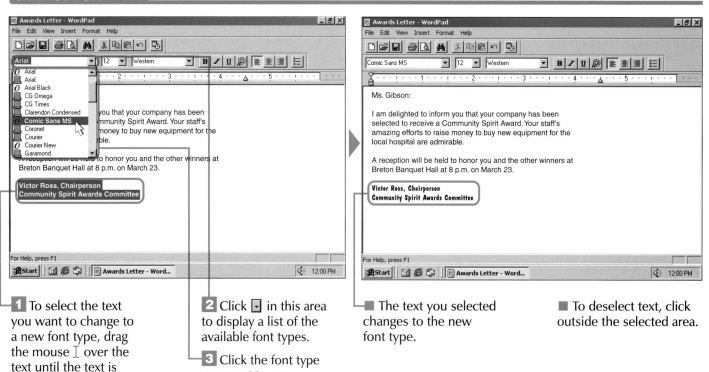

1 To select the text you want to change to a new font type, drag the mouse I over the text until the text is highlighted.

2 Click 🔽 in this area to display a list of the available font types.

3 Click the font type you want to use.

■ The text you selected changes to the new font type.

■ To deselect text, click outside the selected area.

CHANGE FONT SIZE

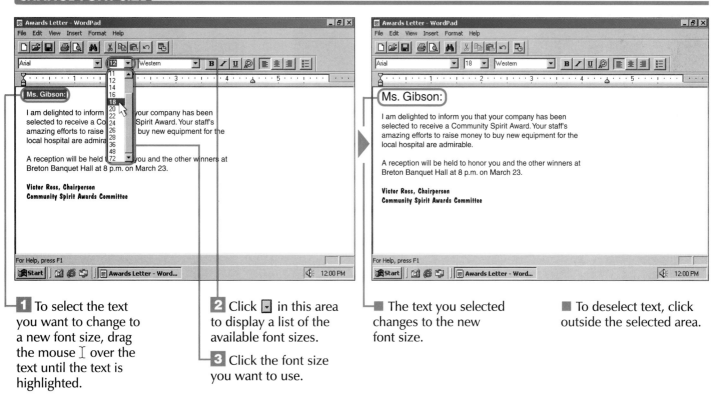

1 To select the text you want to change to a new font size, drag the mouse I over the text until the text is highlighted.

2 Click ⊡ in this area to display a list of the available font sizes.

3 Click the font size you want to use.

■ The text you selected changes to the new font size.

■ To deselect text, click outside the selected area.

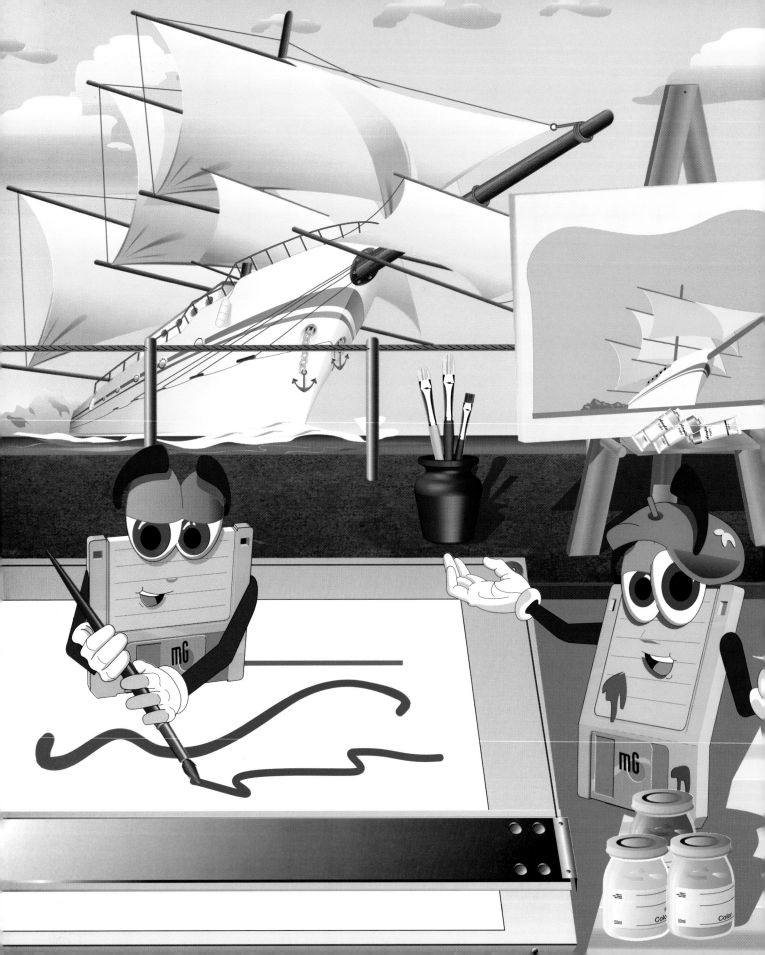

CHAPTER 3

CREATE PICTURES

Feeling artistic? This chapter will teach you how to create pictures on your computer using the Paint program.

START PAINT

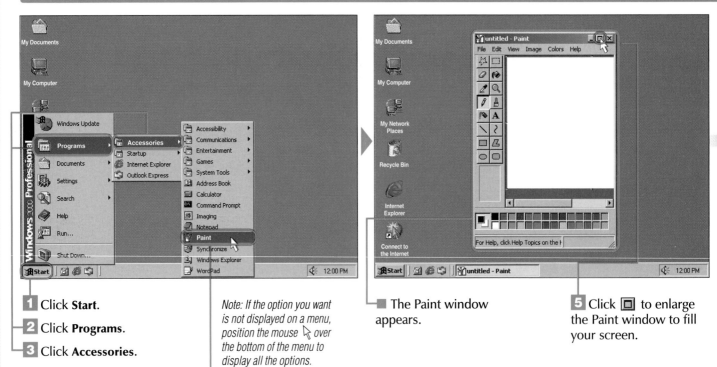

1 Click **Start**.

2 Click **Programs**.

3 Click **Accessories**.

Note: If the option you want is not displayed on a menu, position the mouse ⬎ over the bottom of the menu to display all the options.

4 Click **Paint**.

■ The Paint window appears.

5 Click ▣ to enlarge the Paint window to fill your screen.

What can I do with the pictures I draw in Paint?

You can place the pictures you draw in Paint in other programs. For example, you can add your company logo to a business letter you created in WordPad.

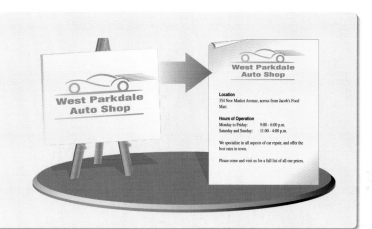

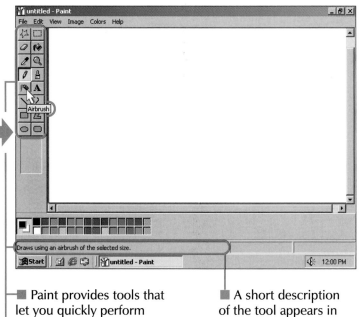

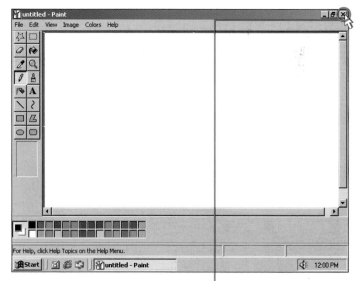

■ Paint provides tools that let you quickly perform tasks.

6 To display a description of a tool, position the mouse � over the tool (example: ▨). After a moment, the name of the tool appears.

■ A short description of the tool appears in this area.

You can exit Paint when you finish using the program.

1 Before exiting Paint, save any changes you made to the picture. To save your changes, see page 47.

2 Click ☒ to exit Paint.

You can draw shapes such as circles and squares in various colors.

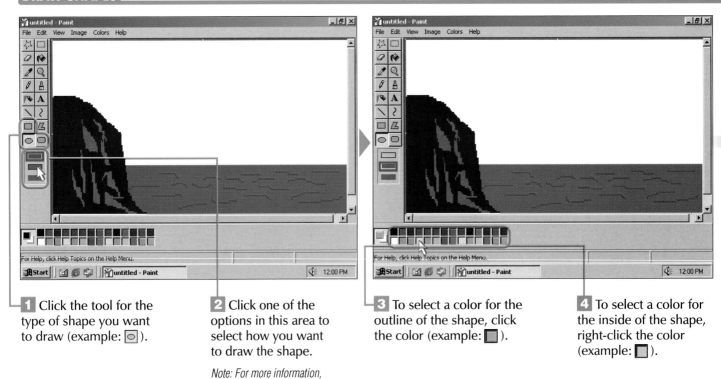

1 Click the tool for the type of shape you want to draw (example: ⬭).

2 Click one of the options in this area to select how you want to draw the shape.

Note: For more information, see the top of page 43.

3 To select a color for the outline of the shape, click the color (example: ■).

4 To select a color for the inside of the shape, right-click the color (example: ▢).

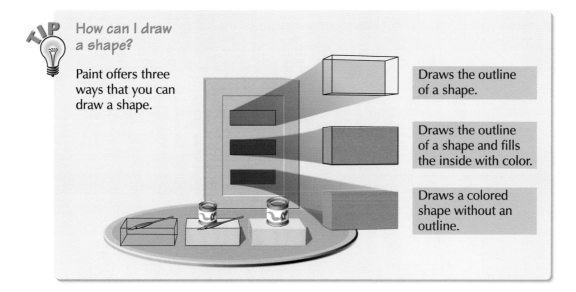

How can I draw a shape?

Paint offers three ways that you can draw a shape.

Draws the outline of a shape.

Draws the outline of a shape and fills the inside with color.

Draws a colored shape without an outline.

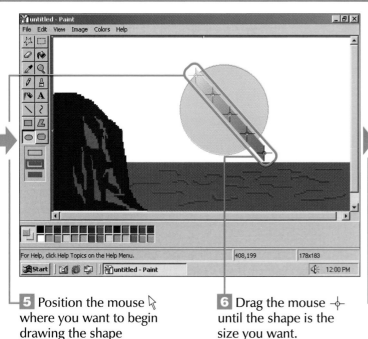

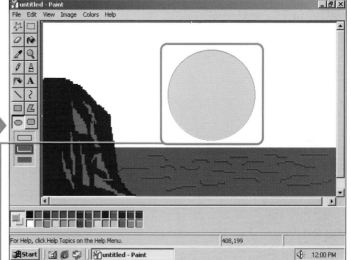

5 Position the mouse ⬚ where you want to begin drawing the shape (⬚ changes to ✛).

6 Drag the mouse ✛ until the shape is the size you want.

Note: To draw a perfect circle or square, press and hold down the **Shift** *key as you perform step 6.*

■ The shape appears.

You can draw straight, wavy and curved lines in various colors.

DRAW LINES

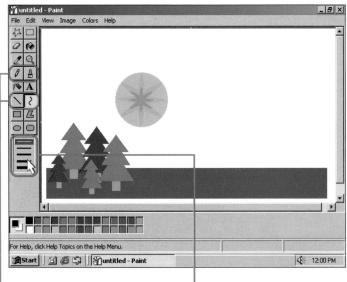

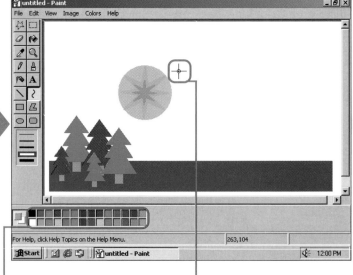

1 Click the tool for the type of line you want to draw (example: ⟨?⟩).

Note: For more information, see the top of page 45.

2 To select a line thickness, click one of the options in this area.

Note: The ✏ tool does not provide any line thickness options. The 𝘼 tool provides a different set of options.

3 To select a color for the line, click the color (example: ▦).

4 Position the mouse ▷ where you want to begin drawing the line (▷ changes to ✛, ⟋ or ✛).

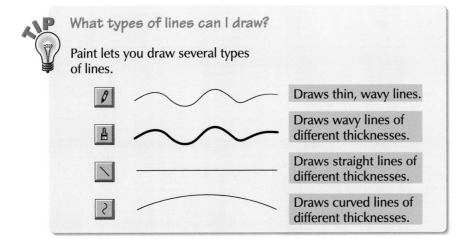

What types of lines can I draw?

Paint lets you draw several types
of lines.

Draws thin, wavy lines.

Draws wavy lines of
different thicknesses.

Draws straight lines of
different thicknesses.

Draws curved lines of
different thicknesses.

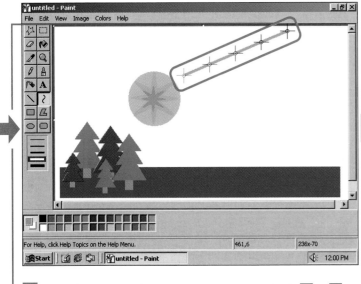

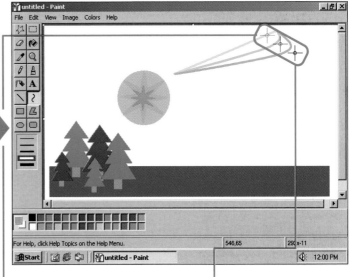

5 Drag the mouse ⊹
until the line is the length
you want.

*Note: When using the ＼ or ✐
tool, you can draw a perfectly
horizontal, vertical or 45-degree
line. To do so, press and hold
down the* **Shift** *key as you
perform step* **5**.

■ If you selected the ⌇
tool in step **1**, you can
now curve the line.

6 To curve the line,
position the mouse ⊹
over the line.

7 Drag the mouse ⊹
until the line curves the
way you want. Then
immediately click the left
mouse button again to
complete the curved line.

When choosing a color for the eraser, select a color that matches the background color of your picture.

ERASE PART OF A PICTURE

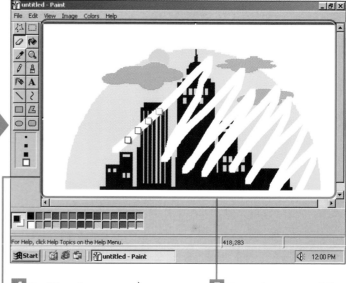

1 Click 🖉.

2 Click the size of eraser you want to use.

3 Right-click a color for the eraser (example: ☐).

4 Position the mouse ⬚ where you want to start erasing (⬚ changes to ☐).

5 Drag the mouse ☐ over the area you want to erase.

Note: To immediately undo the change, press and hold down the **Ctrl** *key and then press the* **Z** *key.*

You should save your picture to store it for future use. This allows you to later review and make changes to the picture.

You should regularly save changes you make to a picture to avoid losing your work.

SAVE A PICTURE

1 Click **File**.

2 Click **Save**.

■ The Save As dialog box appears.

Note: If you previously saved the picture, the Save As dialog box will not appear since you have already named the picture.

3 Type a name for the picture.

■ This area shows the location where Paint will store the picture. You can click this area to change the location.

4 Click **Save**.

You can open a saved picture and display the picture on your screen. This allows you to view and make changes to the picture.

OPEN A PICTURE

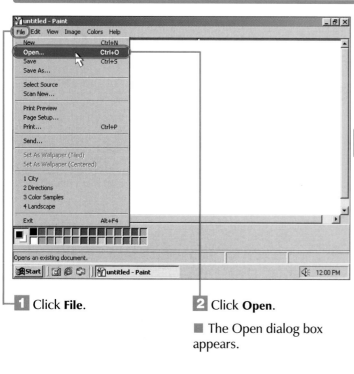

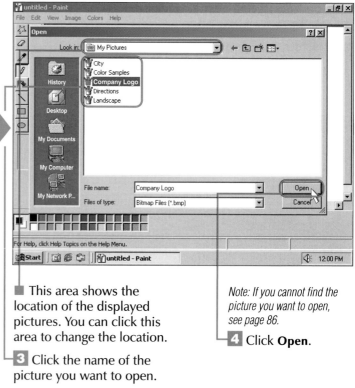

1 Click **File**.

2 Click **Open**.

■ The Open dialog box appears.

■ This area shows the location of the displayed pictures. You can click this area to change the location.

3 Click the name of the picture you want to open.

Note: If you cannot find the picture you want to open, see page 86.

4 Click **Open**.

Can I work with two pictures at the same time?

Paint lets you work with only one picture at a time. If you are currently working with a picture, save the picture before opening another. For information on saving a picture, see page 47.

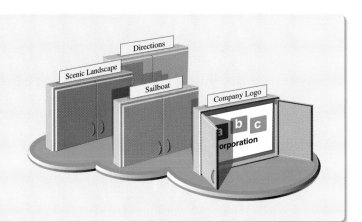

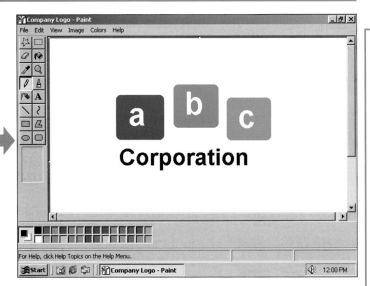

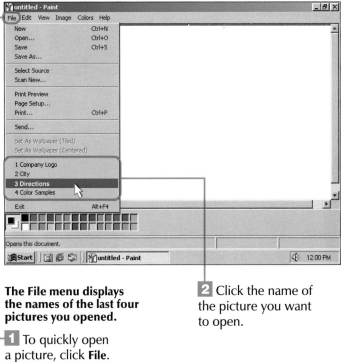

■ Paint opens the picture and displays it on your screen. You can now view and make changes to the picture.

The File menu displays the names of the last four pictures you opened.

1 To quickly open a picture, click **File**.

2 Click the name of the picture you want to open.

History ×

▼ Go

Sales Budget

Map to
Chicago

Marketing
Strategies

Ad Campaign

Project
Analysis

Conference

Employee
Guidelines

Memo to Sales
Director

Corporation
Logo

Sales Report

71.0 KB | 💻 My Computer

CHAPTER 4

VIEW FILES

Are you looking for a file? This chapter shows you how to view the information stored on your computer.

VIEW CONTENTS OF YOUR COMPUTER

You can easily view the folders and files stored on your computer.

Like a filing cabinet, your computer uses folders to organize information.

VIEW CONTENTS OF YOUR COMPUTER

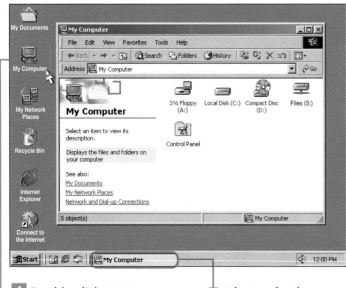

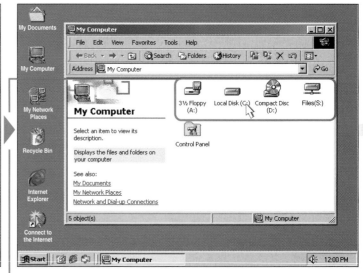

1 Double-click **My Computer** to view the contents of your computer.

■ The My Computer window appears.

■ A button for the open window appears on the taskbar.

■ These items represent drives on your computer and the network.

2 To display the contents of a drive, double-click the drive.

Note: If you want to view the contents of a floppy or CD-ROM drive, make sure you insert a floppy disk or CD-ROM disc before performing step 2.

■ The contents of the drive appear.

52

TIP

What do the icons in the My Computer window represent?

The My Computer window displays icons to represent drives on your computer and the network.

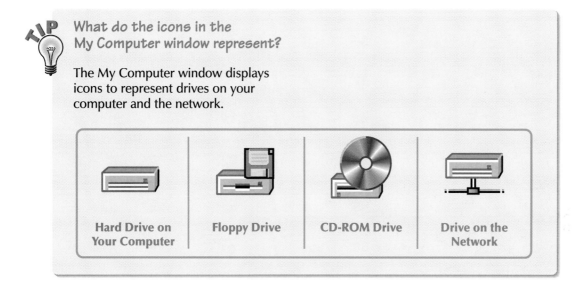

Hard Drive on Your Computer | **Floppy Drive** | **CD-ROM Drive** | **Drive on the Network**

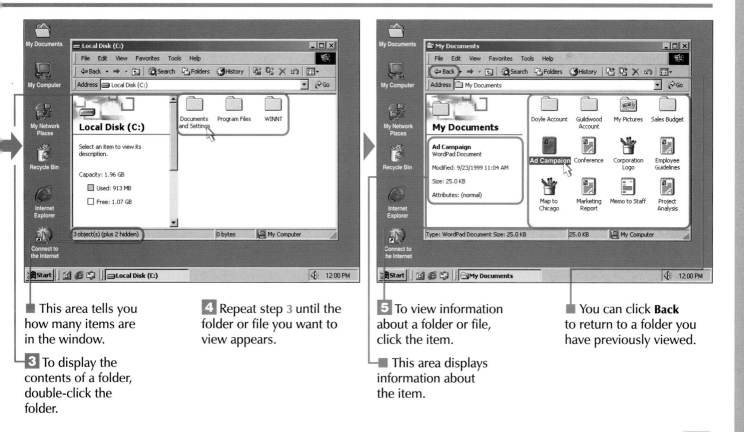

■ This area tells you how many items are in the window.

3 To display the contents of a folder, double-click the folder.

4 Repeat step **3** until the folder or file you want to view appears.

5 To view information about a folder or file, click the item.

■ This area displays information about the item.

■ You can click **Back** to return to a folder you have previously viewed.

You can change the appearance of items in a window. The appearance you select determines the information you will see in the window.

CHANGE APPEARANCE OF ITEMS

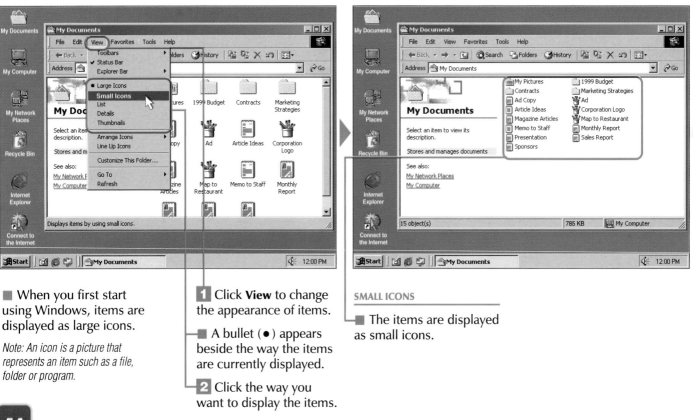

■ When you first start using Windows, items are displayed as large icons.

Note: An icon is a picture that represents an item such as a file, folder or program.

1 Click **View** to change the appearance of items.

■ A bullet (●) appears beside the way the items are currently displayed.

2 Click the way you want to display the items.

SMALL ICONS

■ The items are displayed as small icons.

What is the Thumbnails view?

The Thumbnails view allows you to display a miniature version of each picture file in the window. Icons for other types of files are displayed in boxes. The Thumbnails view is not available in some windows.

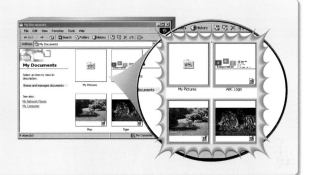

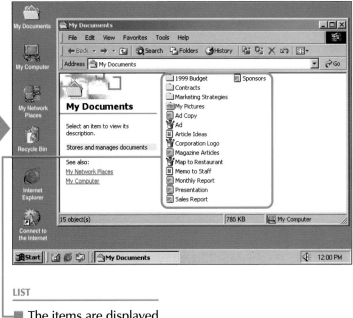

LIST

■ The items are displayed as small icons arranged in a list.

DETAILS

■ Information about each item is displayed, such as the name, size and type of item.

You can sort the items displayed in a window. This can help you find files and folders more easily.

SORT ITEMS

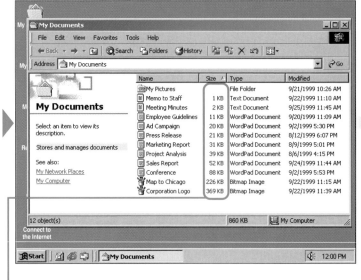

■ When you first start using Windows, items are sorted alphabetically by name.

1 Click the heading for the column you want to use to sort the items.

Note: If the headings are not displayed, perform steps 1 and 2 on page 54, selecting Details in step 2.

■ To sort the items in the reverse order, click the heading again.

SORT BY SIZE

■ The items are sorted by size.

How does Windows
measure the size of files?

The size of each file is
measured in kilobytes (KB).
An average letter created in
WordPad is approximately
5 KB.

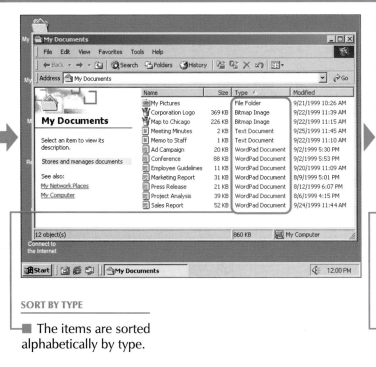

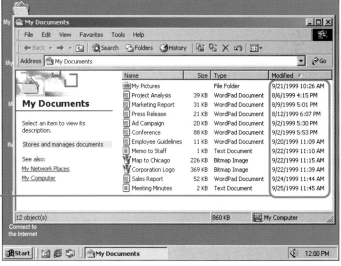

SORT BY TYPE

■ The items are sorted
alphabetically by type.

SORT BY DATE

■ The items are sorted
by the date they were
last saved.

USING WINDOWS EXPLORER

Windows Explorer shows the location of every folder and file on your computer.

You can move, rename and delete files in Windows Explorer as you would in a My Computer window.

USING WINDOWS EXPLORER

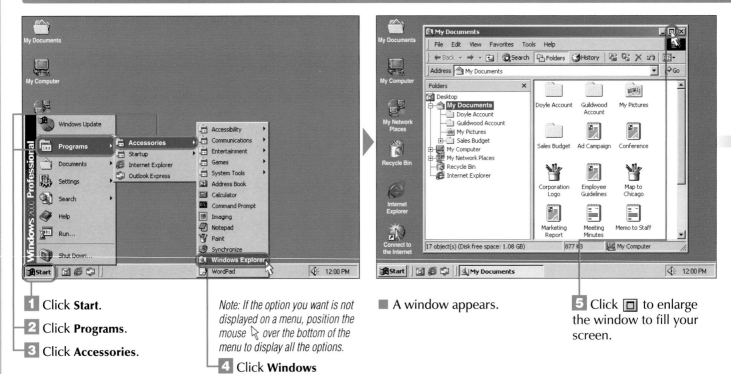

1 Click **Start**.

2 Click **Programs**.

3 Click **Accessories**.

Note: If the option you want is not displayed on a menu, position the mouse Ⓚ over the bottom of the menu to display all the options.

4 Click **Windows Explorer**.

■ A window appears.

5 Click ▫ to enlarge the window to fill your screen.

Why don't the contents of some folders appear when I click the name of the folder?

Some folders contain important files that help keep your computer working properly. Windows does not automatically display the contents of these folders to prevent you from accidentally moving or deleting the files. To view the contents of the folder, click **Show Files** in the window.

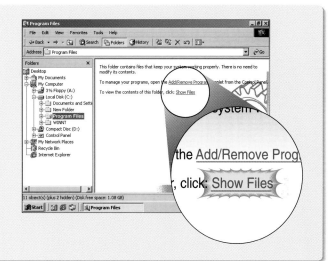

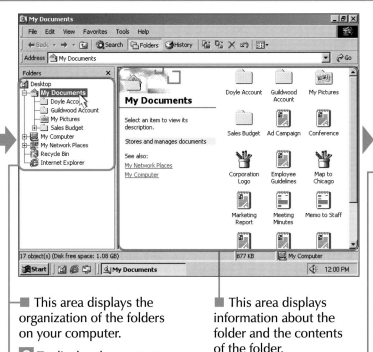

■ This area displays the organization of the folders on your computer.

6 To display the contents of a folder, click the name of the folder.

■ This area displays information about the folder and the contents of the folder.

7 To view information about an item in the folder, click the item. The item is highlighted.

■ This area displays information about the item you selected.

Note: To once again display information about all the items in the folder, click a blank area on the right side of the window.

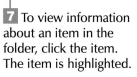

A folder may contain other folders. You can easily display or hide these folders at any time.

DISPLAY HIDDEN FOLDERS

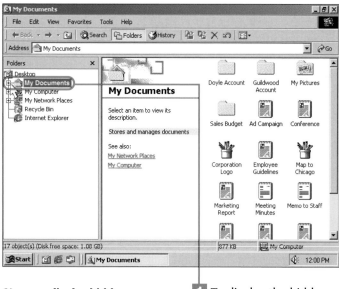

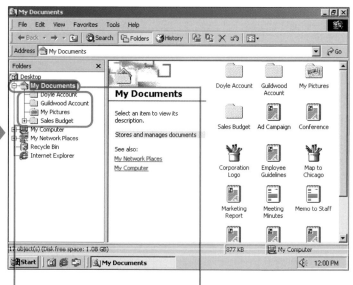

You can display hidden folders to view more of the information stored on your computer.

1 To display the hidden folders within a folder, click the plus sign (⊞) beside the folder.

■ The hidden folders appear.

■ The plus sign (⊞) beside the folder changes to a minus sign (⊟). This indicates that all the folders within the folder are now displayed.

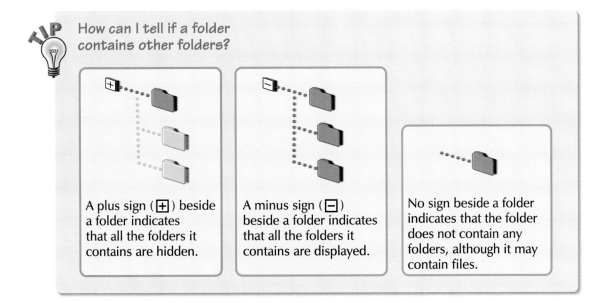

How can I tell if a folder contains other folders?

A plus sign (⊞) beside a folder indicates that all the folders it contains are hidden.

A minus sign (⊟) beside a folder indicates that all the folders it contains are displayed.

No sign beside a folder indicates that the folder does not contain any folders, although it may contain files.

HIDE FOLDERS

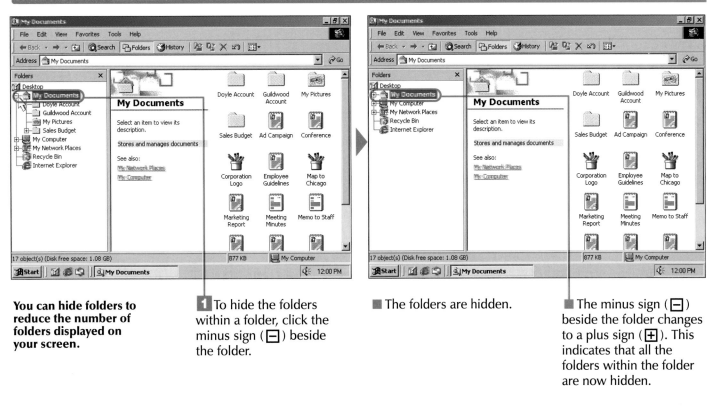

You can hide folders to reduce the number of folders displayed on your screen.

◼ 1 To hide the folders within a folder, click the minus sign (⊟) beside the folder.

◼ The folders are hidden.

◼ The minus sign (⊟) beside the folder changes to a plus sign (⊞). This indicates that all the folders within the folder are now hidden.

Annual Staff Picnic

Saturday, July 17, 1999
10:30 am - 6:00 pm
Garden Gate Park

All employees are invited to
bring their families out for a
fun-filled day at the park. There
will be plenty of food and lots
of exciting games.

CHAPTER 5

WORK WITH FILES

Do you want to learn how to open, move or copy a file? Do you want to delete a file you no longer need? Learn how to manage your files in this chapter.

You can open a file to display its contents on your screen. This lets you review and make changes to the file.

OPEN A FILE

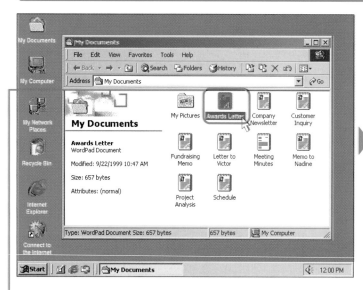

1 Double-click the file you want to open.

■ The file opens. You can review and make changes to the file.

2 When you finish working with the file, click ✕ to close the file.

Windows remembers the files you most recently used. You can quickly open any of these files.

OPEN A RECENTLY USED FILE

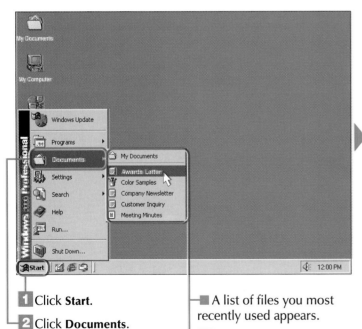

1 Click **Start**.

2 Click **Documents**.

■ A list of files you most recently used appears.

3 Click the file you want to open.

*Note: You can click **My Documents** to open the My Documents folder. Many programs automatically store documents you create in this folder.*

■ The file opens. You can review and make changes to the file.

4 When you finish working with the file, click ☒ to close the file.

Before working with files, you must first select the files you want to work with. Selected files appear highlighted on your screen.

You can select folders the same way you select files. Selecting a folder will select all the files in the folder.

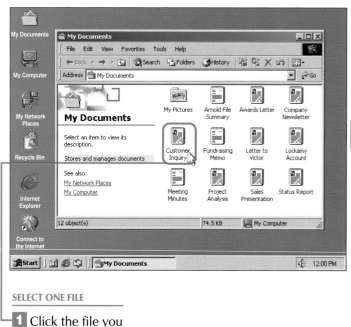

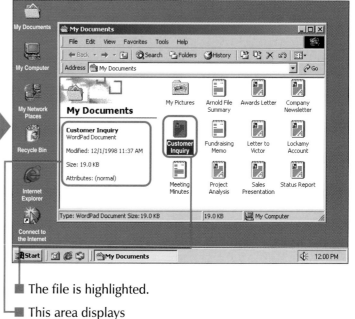

SELECT ONE FILE

1 Click the file you want to select.

■ The file is highlighted.

■ This area displays information about the file.

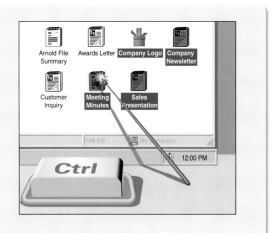

How do I deselect files?

To deselect all of the files in a window, click a blank area in the window.

To deselect one file from a group of selected files, press and hold down the **Ctrl** key as you click the file you want to deselect.

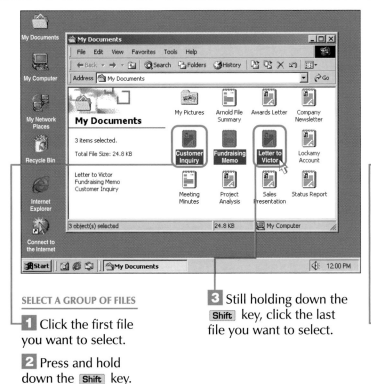

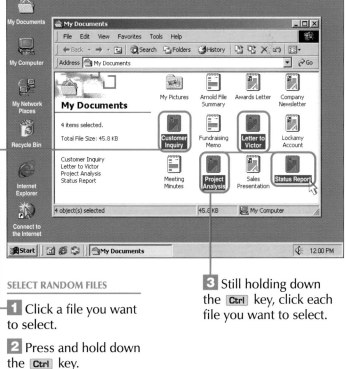

SELECT A GROUP OF FILES

1 Click the first file you want to select.

2 Press and hold down the **Shift** key.

3 Still holding down the **Shift** key, click the last file you want to select.

SELECT RANDOM FILES

1 Click a file you want to select.

2 Press and hold down the **Ctrl** key.

3 Still holding down the **Ctrl** key, click each file you want to select.

You can give a file a new name to better describe the contents of the file. This can make the file easier to find.

Company Picnic

Announcement

Date: Saturday, July 22, 2000
Time: 10:30 AM - 6:00 PM
Venue: Garden Gate Park

All employees are invited to bring their families out for a fun-filled day at the park. There will be plenty of food and lots of exciting games and activities for the whole family.

RENAME A FILE

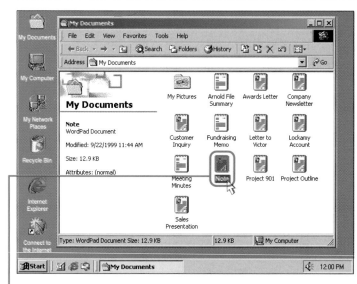

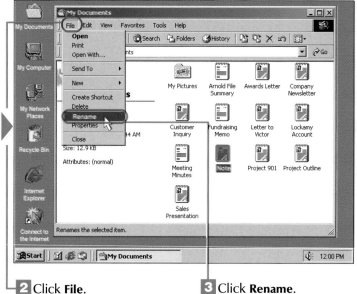

1 Click the file you want to rename.

2 Click **File**.

3 Click **Rename**.

Can I rename a folder?

You should only rename folders that you have created. To rename a folder, perform the steps below, selecting the folder you want to rename in step **1**.

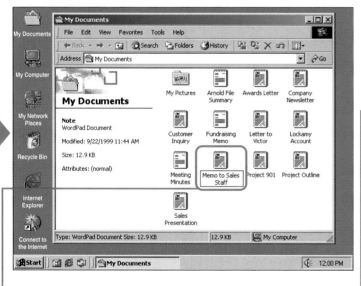

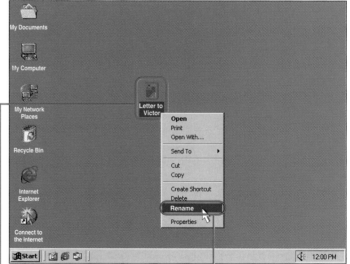

■ The name of the file appears in a box.

4 Type a new name for the file and then press the `Enter` key.

*Note: A file name cannot contain the \ /: * ? " < > or | characters.*

You can easily rename a file on your desktop.

1 Right-click the file you want to rename. A menu appears.

2 Click **Rename**.

3 Type a new name and then press the `Enter` key.

You can create a new folder to help you better organize the information stored on your computer. Creating a folder is like placing a new folder in a filing cabinet.

CREATE A NEW FOLDER

1 Display the contents of the folder where you want to place the new folder.

Note: To browse through the contents of your computer, see page 52.

2 Click **File**.

3 Click **New**.

4 Click **Folder**.

TIP

How can creating new folders help me organize the information on my computer?

You can create as many new folders as you need to develop a filing system that works for you. You can then organize your files by moving them to the new folders. To move files, see page 74.

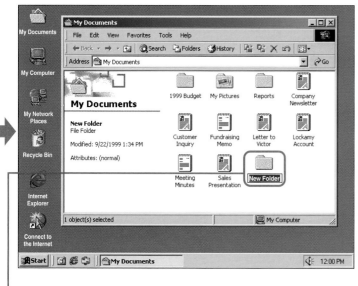

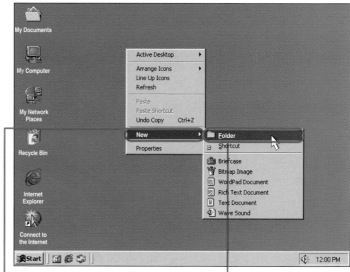

■ The new folder appears, displaying a temporary name (**New Folder**).

■5 Type a name for the new folder and then press the **Enter** key.

*Note: A folder name cannot contain the \ /: * ? " < > or | characters.*

You can create a new folder on your desktop.

■1 Right-click an empty area on your desktop. A menu appears.

■2 Click **New**.

■3 Click **Folder**.

■4 Type a name for the new folder and then press the **Enter** key.

You can instantly create, name and store a new file in the appropriate location without starting any programs.

You can focus on the organization of your files rather than the programs you need to accomplish your tasks.

CREATE A NEW FILE

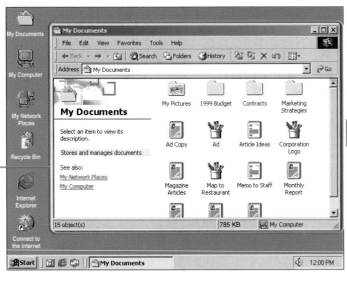

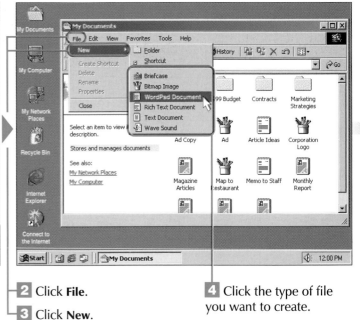

1 Display the contents of the folder where you want to place a new file.

2 Click **File**.

3 Click **New**.

4 Click the type of file you want to create.

TIP

What types of files can I create?

The types of files you can create depend on the programs installed on your computer. By default, Windows allows you to create several types of files, such as images and text documents.

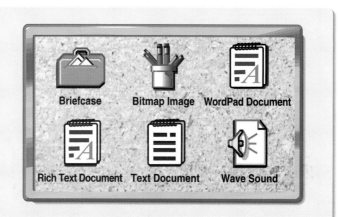

Briefcase   Bitmap Image   WordPad Document

Rich Text Document   Text Document   Wave Sound

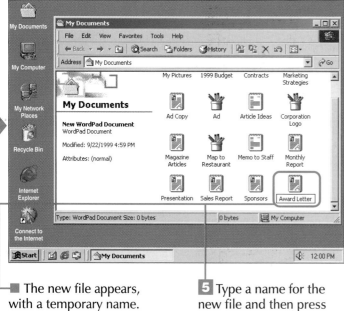

■ The new file appears, with a temporary name.

5 Type a name for the new file and then press the Enter key.

You can create a new file on your desktop.

1 Right-click a blank area on your desktop. A menu appears.

2 Click **New**.

3 Click the type of file you want to create.

4 Type a name for the new file and then press the Enter key.

MOVE AND COPY FILES

You can organize the files stored on your computer by moving or copying them to new locations.

Organizing files on your computer is similar to organizing files in a filing cabinet.

MOVE FILES

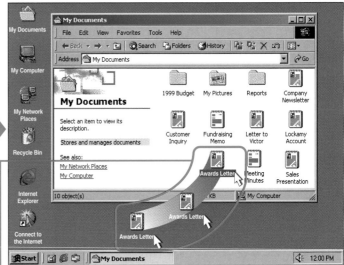

1 Position the mouse ⍺ over the file you want to move.

■ To move more than one file, select all the files you want to move. Then position the mouse ⍺ over one of the files.

Note: To select multiple files, see page 67.

2 Drag the file to a new location on your computer.

74

TIP

What is the difference between moving and copying a file?

Move a File

When you move a file, you place the file in a new location on your computer.

Copy a File

When you copy a file, you make an exact copy of the file and then place the copy in a new location. This lets you store the file in two locations.

COPY FILES

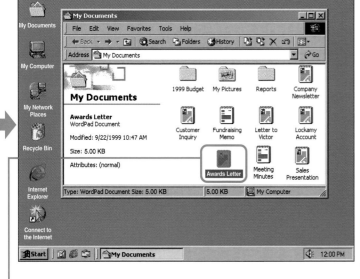

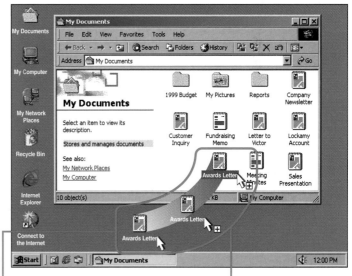

■ The file moves to the new location.

Note: You can move folders the same way you move files. When you move a folder, all the files in the folder also move.

1 Position the mouse ▷ over the file you want to copy.

2 Press and hold down the `Ctrl` key.

3 Still holding down the `Ctrl` key, drag the file to a new location.

You can make an exact copy of a file and then place the copy on a floppy disk. This is useful if you want to give a colleague a copy of the file.

COPY A FILE TO A FLOPPY DISK

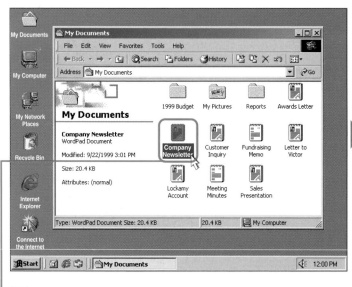

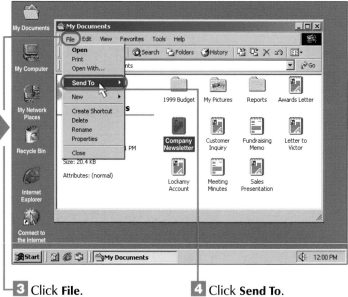

1 Insert a floppy disk into the floppy drive.

2 Click the file you want to copy to a floppy disk.

■ To copy more than one file, select all the files you want to copy.

Note: To select multiple files, see page 67.

3 Click **File**.

4 Click **Send To**.

TIP

How can I protect the information on my floppy disks?

You should keep floppy disks away from magnets, which can damage the information stored on the disks. Also be careful not to spill liquids, such as coffee or soda, on the disks.

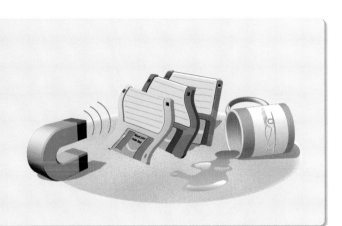

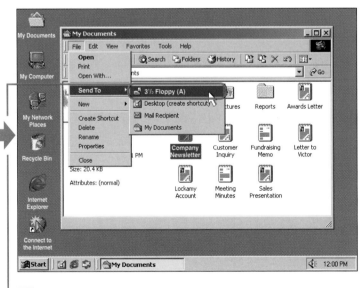

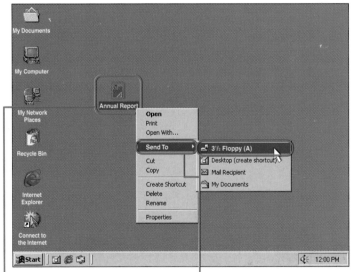

5 Click the drive that contains the floppy disk.

■ Windows places a copy of the file on the floppy disk.

Note: You can copy a folder to a floppy disk the same way you copy a file. When you copy a folder, all the files in the folder are also copied.

You can copy a file on your desktop to a floppy disk.

1 Insert a floppy disk into the floppy drive.

2 Right-click the file you want to copy to a floppy disk. A menu appears.

3 Click **Send To**.

4 Click the drive that contains the floppy disk.

You can delete a file you no longer need.

Before you delete a file, consider the value of your work. Do not delete a file unless you are certain you no longer need the file.

DELETE A FILE

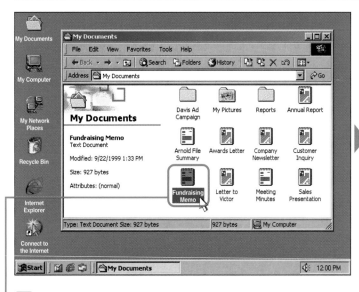

1 Click the file you want to delete.

■ To delete more than one file, select the files.

Note: To select multiple files, see page 67.

2 Press the Delete key.

■ The Confirm File Delete dialog box appears.

3 Click **Yes** to delete the file.

Can I delete any file on my computer?

Make sure you only delete files that you have created. Do not delete any files that Windows or other programs require to operate.

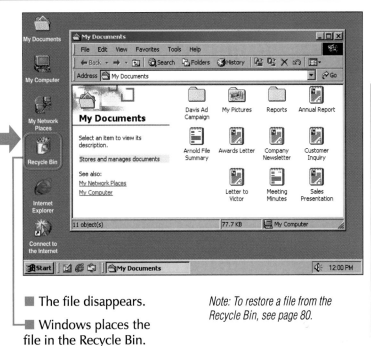

■ The file disappears.

■ Windows places the file in the Recycle Bin.

Note: To restore a file from the Recycle Bin, see page 80.

You can delete a folder and all the files it contains.

1 Click the folder you want to delete.

2 Press the Delete key.

■ The Confirm Folder Delete dialog box appears.

3 Click **Yes** to delete the folder.

The Recycle Bin stores all the files you have deleted. You can easily restore any of these files.

RESTORE A DELETED FILE

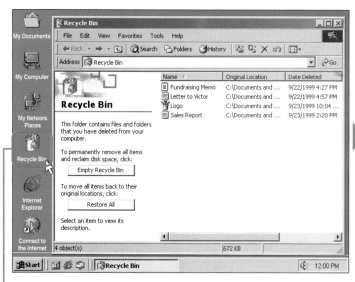

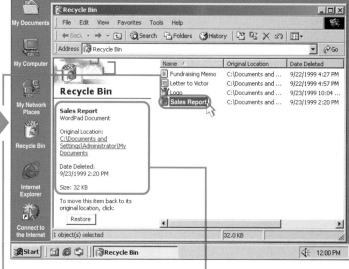

1 Double-click **Recycle Bin** to display all the files you have deleted.

■ The Recycle Bin window appears, displaying all the files you have deleted.

2 Click the file you want to restore.

■ To restore more than one file, select the files.

Note: To select multiple files, see page 67.

■ This area displays information about the file you selected.

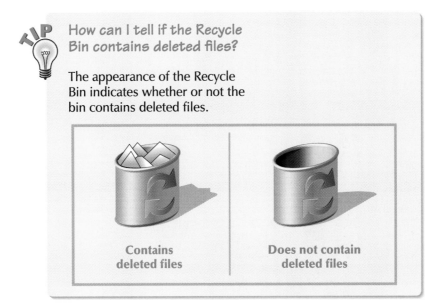

How can I tell if the Recycle Bin contains deleted files?

The appearance of the Recycle Bin indicates whether or not the bin contains deleted files.

Contains deleted files

Does not contain deleted files

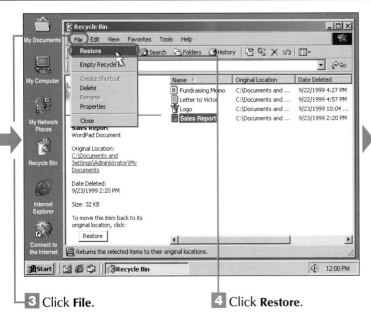

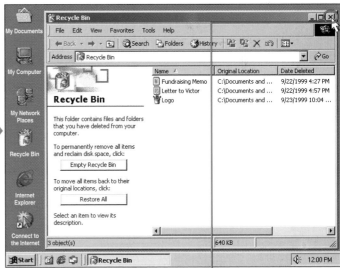

3 Click **File**.

4 Click **Restore**.

■ The file disappears from the Recycle Bin window. Windows places the file back in its original location.

5 Click ⊠ to close the Recycle Bin window.

Note: You can restore folders the same way you restore files. When you restore a folder, all the files in the folder are also restored.

You can create more free space on your computer by permanently removing all the files from the Recycle Bin.

EMPTY THE RECYCLE BIN

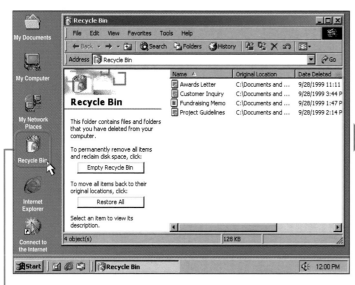

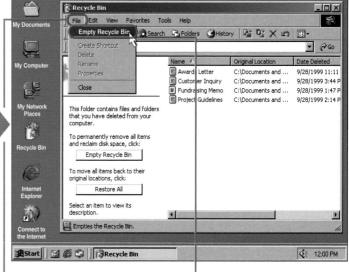

1 Double-click **Recycle Bin** to display all the files you have deleted.

■ The Recycle Bin window appears, displaying all the files you have deleted.

2 Click **File**.

3 Click **Empty Recycle Bin**.

What if the Recycle Bin contains a file I may need?

Before emptying the Recycle Bin, make sure it does not contain files you may need in the future. To restore a file you may need, see page 80. Once you empty the Recycle Bin, the files are permanently removed from your computer and cannot be restored.

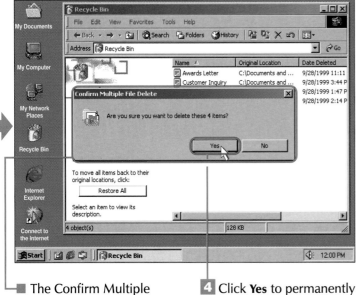

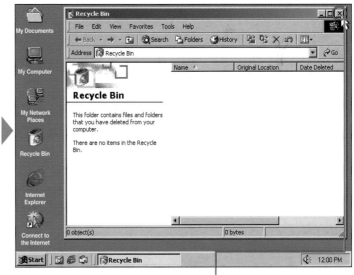

■ The Confirm Multiple File Delete dialog box appears.

4 Click **Yes** to permanently delete all the files.

■ All the files are permanently deleted from your computer.

5 Click ⊠ to close the Recycle Bin window.

You can produce a paper copy of a file stored on your computer. Before printing, make sure your printer is turned on and contains paper.

PRINT A FILE

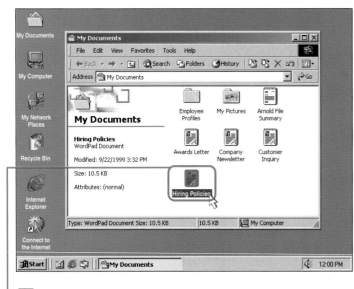

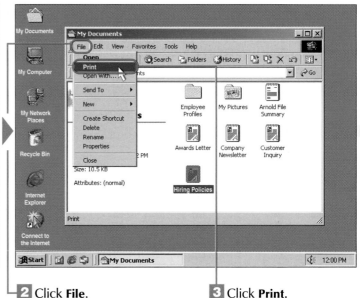

1 Click the file you want to print.

■ To print more than one file, select the files.

Note: To select multiple files, see page 67.

2 Click **File**.

3 Click **Print**.

What types of printers can I use to print my files?

Windows works with many types of printers. There are two common types of printers.

Ink-jet

An ink-jet printer produces documents that are suitable for routine business and personal use.

Laser

A laser printer is faster and produces higher-quality documents than an ink-jet printer, but is more expensive.

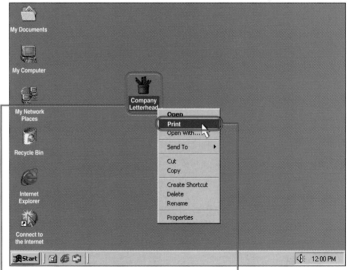

■ When you print a file, the printer icon (🖨) appears in this area. The icon disappears when the file has finished printing.

You can print a file located on your desktop.

1 Right-click the file you want to print. A menu appears.

2 Click **Print**.

If you cannot remember the exact name or location of a file you want to work with, you can have Windows search for the file.

SEARCH FOR FILES

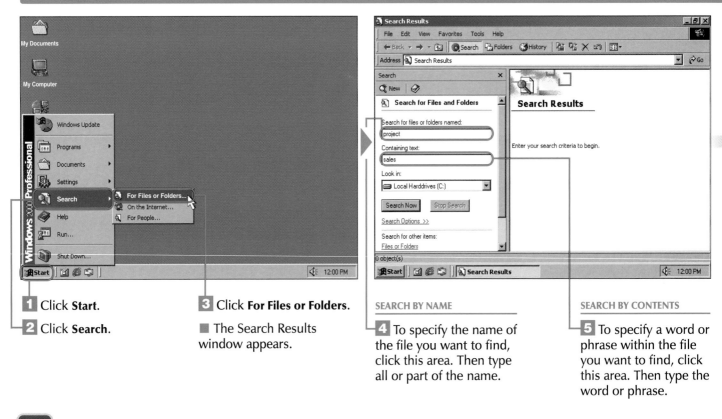

1 Click **Start**.

2 Click **Search**.

3 Click **For Files or Folders**.

■ The Search Results window appears.

SEARCH BY NAME

4 To specify the name of the file you want to find, click this area. Then type all or part of the name.

SEARCH BY CONTENTS

5 To specify a word or phrase within the file you want to find, click this area. Then type the word or phrase.

Can I search for a file if I know
only part of the file name?

If you search for part of a file
name, Windows will find all the
files and folders with names that
contain the word you specified.
For example, searching for the
word "report" will find every file
or folder with a name containing
the word "report".

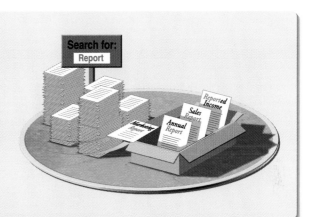

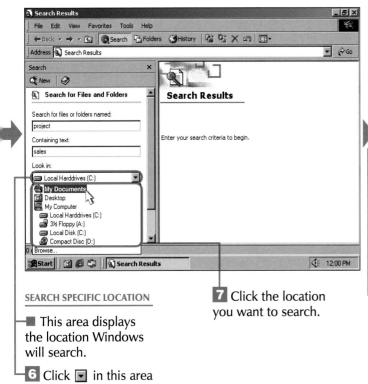

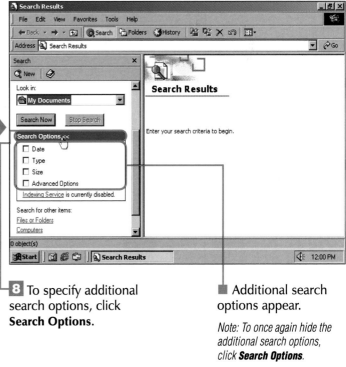

SEARCH SPECIFIC LOCATION

■ This area displays
the location Windows
will search.

6 Click ■ in this area
to select a different
location.

7 Click the location
you want to search.

8 To specify additional
search options, click
Search Options.

■ Additional search
options appear.

*Note: To once again hide the
additional search options,
click **Search Options**.*

CONTINUED

SEARCH FOR FILES (CONTINUED)

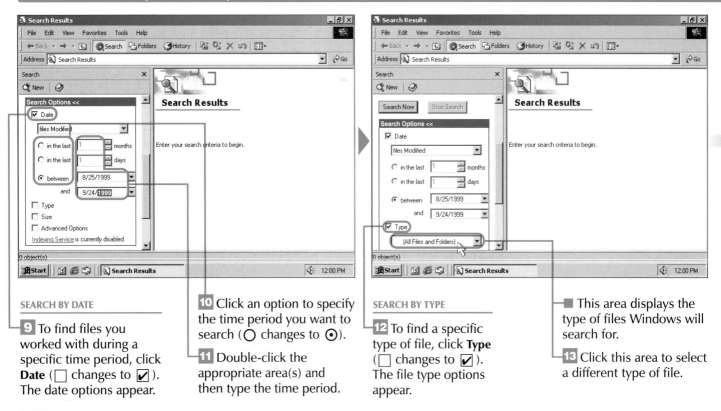

SEARCH BY DATE

9 To find files you worked with during a specific time period, click **Date** (☐ changes to ☑). The date options appear.

10 Click an option to specify the time period you want to search (○ changes to ⊙).

11 Double-click the appropriate area(s) and then type the time period.

SEARCH BY TYPE

12 To find a specific type of file, click **Type** (☐ changes to ☑). The file type options appear.

■ This area displays the type of files Windows will search for.

13 Click this area to select a different type of file.

How can I find all the programs on my computer?

To find all the programs on your computer, perform steps 1 to 8 starting on page 86. Then perform steps 12 to 15 below, selecting **Application** in step 14.

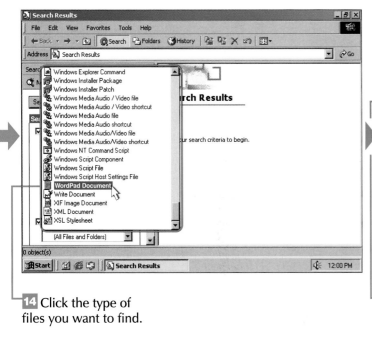

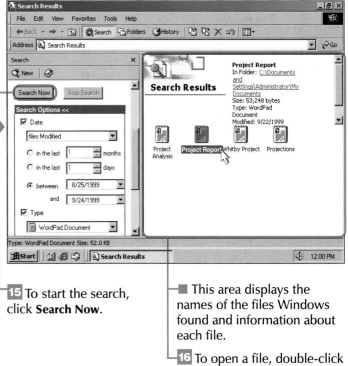

14 Click the type of files you want to find.

15 To start the search, click **Search Now**.

■ This area displays the names of the files Windows found and information about each file.

16 To open a file, double-click the name of the file.

You can add a shortcut to the desktop to provide a quick way of opening a file you use regularly.

ADD A SHORTCUT TO THE DESKTOP

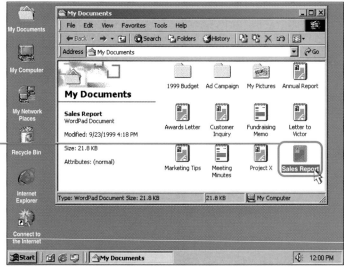

1 Click the file you want to create a shortcut to.

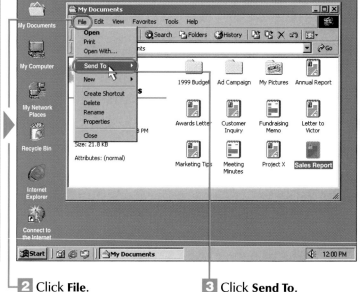

2 Click **File**.

3 Click **Send To**.

How do I rename or delete a shortcut?

You can rename or delete a shortcut the same way you would rename or delete any file. Renaming or deleting a shortcut does not affect the original file. For information on renaming a file, see page 68. For information on deleting a file, see page 78.

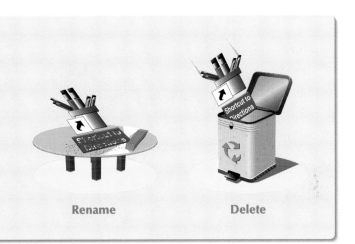

Rename   Delete

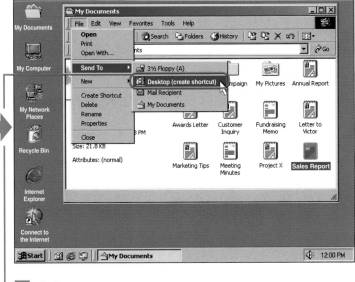

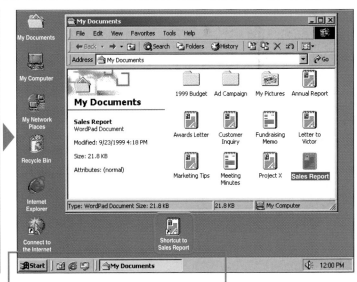

■ 4 Click **Desktop (create shortcut)**.

■ The shortcut appears on the desktop.

■ You can tell the difference between the shortcut and the original file because the shortcut displays an arrow ().

■ You can double-click the shortcut to open the file.

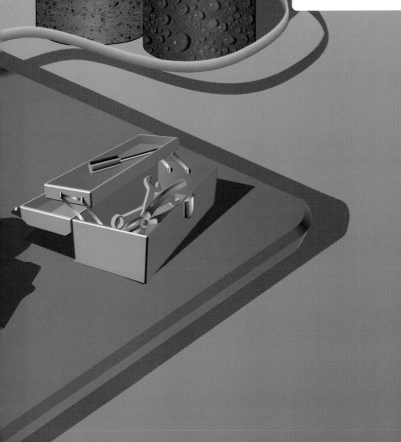

CHAPTER 6

CUSTOMIZE WINDOWS

Would you like to personalize your computer? This chapter shows you how to change the screen colors, set up a screen saver and change the mouse settings to suit your needs.

You should make sure the correct date and time are set in your computer. Windows uses this information to determine when you create and update your documents.

CHANGE THE DATE AND TIME

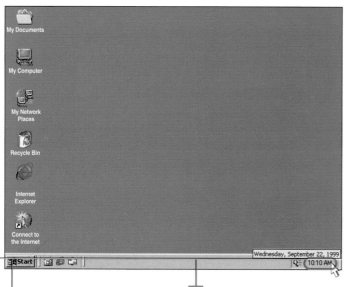

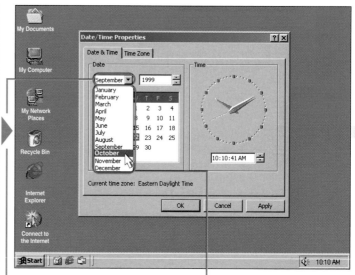

■ This area displays the time set in your computer.

1 To display the date set in your computer, position the mouse ⬚ over this area. A box appears, displaying the date.

2 To change the date or time set in your computer, double-click this area.

■ The Date/Time Properties dialog box appears.

■ This area displays the month set in your computer.

3 To change the month, click this area.

4 Click the correct month.

Will Windows keep track of the date and time even when I turn off my computer?

Your computer has a built-in clock that keeps track of the date and time even when you turn off the computer.

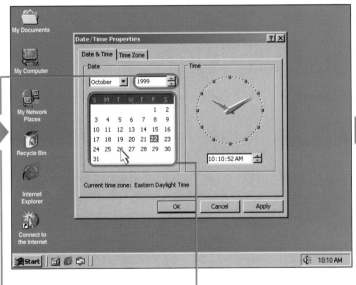

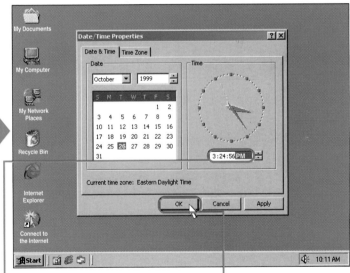

■ This area displays the year set in your computer.

5 To change the year, click ▲ or ▼ in this area until the correct year appears.

■ This area displays the days in the month. The current day is highlighted.

6 To change the day, click the correct day.

■ This area displays the time set in your computer.

7 To change the time, double-click the part of the time you want to change. Then type the correct information.

8 Click **OK** to confirm your changes.

You can decorate your screen by adding wallpaper.

ADD WALLPAPER

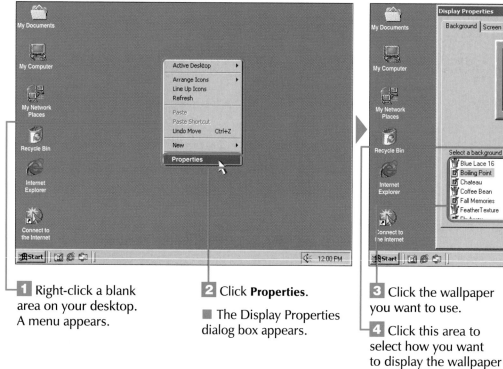

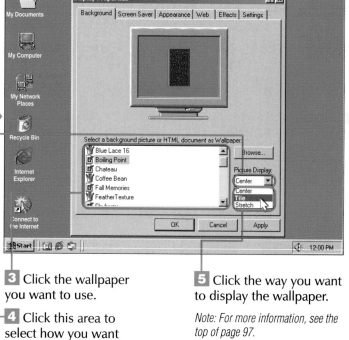

1 Right-click a blank area on your desktop. A menu appears.

2 Click **Properties**.

■ The Display Properties dialog box appears.

3 Click the wallpaper you want to use.

4 Click this area to select how you want to display the wallpaper on your screen.

5 Click the way you want to display the wallpaper.

Note: For more information, see the top of page 97.

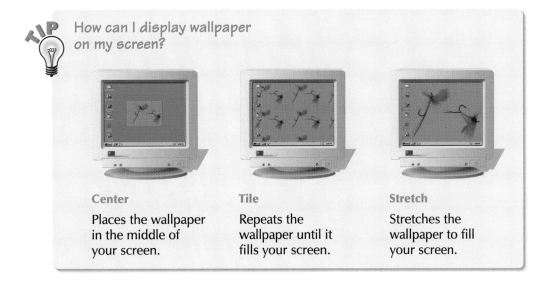

How can I display wallpaper on my screen?

Center

Places the wallpaper in the middle of your screen.

Tile

Repeats the wallpaper until it fills your screen.

Stretch

Stretches the wallpaper to fill your screen.

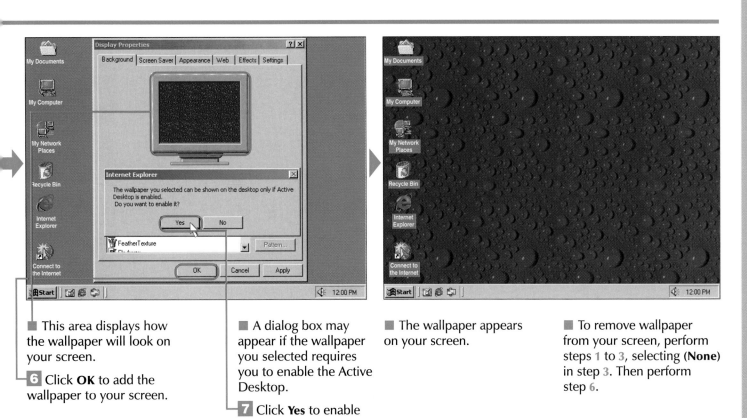

■ This area displays how the wallpaper will look on your screen.

6 Click **OK** to add the wallpaper to your screen.

■ A dialog box may appear if the wallpaper you selected requires you to enable the Active Desktop.

7 Click **Yes** to enable the Active Desktop.

■ The wallpaper appears on your screen.

■ To remove wallpaper from your screen, perform steps 1 to 3, selecting (**None**) in step 3. Then perform step 6.

SET UP A SCREEN SAVER

A screen saver is a moving picture or pattern that appears on the screen when you do not use your computer for a period of time.

Windows allows you to use your logon password with a screen saver to protect your work from unauthorized changes and keep your documents private when you are not at your desk.

SET UP A SCREEN SAVER

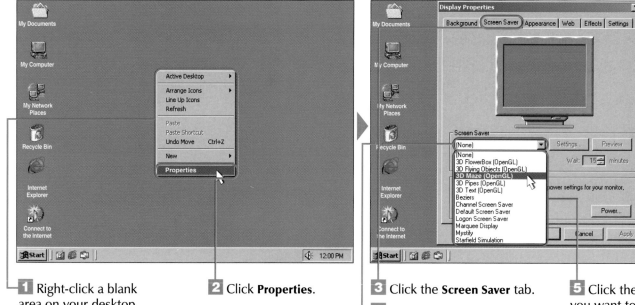

1 Right-click a blank area on your desktop. A menu appears.

2 Click **Properties**.

■ The Display Properties dialog box appears.

3 Click the **Screen Saver** tab.

4 Click this area to display a list of the available screen savers.

5 Click the screen saver you want to use.

How do I remove a screen saver that uses my logon password?

When you move the mouse or press a key to remove a screen saver from your screen, a dialog box appears, telling you the computer is locked. To unlock the computer and remove the screen saver from your screen, perform steps 3 and 4 on page 23.

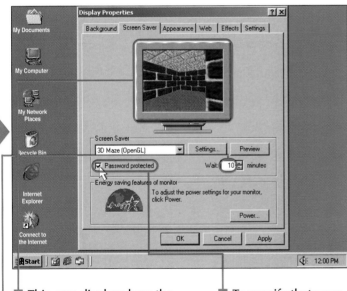

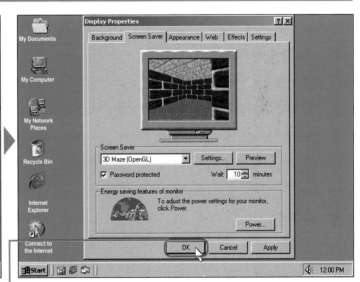

■ This area displays how the screen saver will look on your screen.

6 To change the length of time the computer must be inactive before the screen saver will appear, double-click this area. Then type a new number.

■ To specify that your logon password must be entered to remove the screen saver, click **Password protected** (☐ changes to ☑).

7 Click **OK** to confirm your changes.

■ The screen saver appears when you do not use your computer for the amount of time you specified.

■ You can move the mouse or press a key on the keyboard to remove the screen saver from your screen.

■ To turn off the screen saver, perform steps 1 to 5, selecting (**None**) in step 5. Then perform step 7.

> You can change the colors displayed on your screen to personalize and enhance Windows.

CHANGE SCREEN COLORS

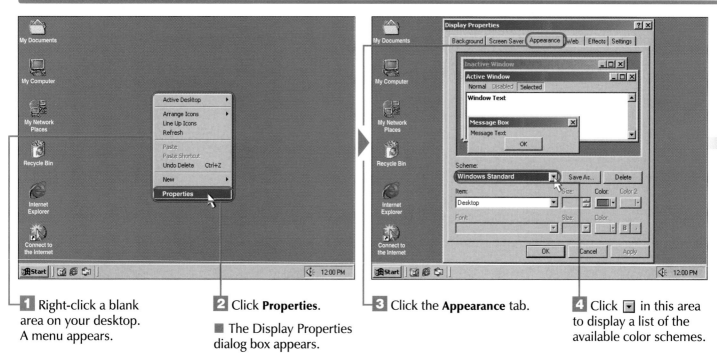

1 Right-click a blank area on your desktop. A menu appears.

2 Click **Properties**.

■ The Display Properties dialog box appears.

3 Click the **Appearance** tab.

4 Click ▼ in this area to display a list of the available color schemes.

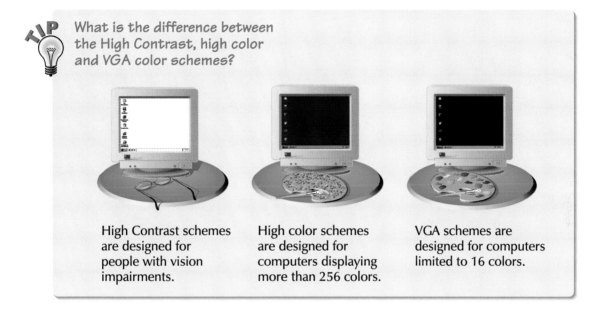

What is the difference between the High Contrast, high color and VGA color schemes?

High Contrast schemes are designed for people with vision impairments.

High color schemes are designed for computers displaying more than 256 colors.

VGA schemes are designed for computers limited to 16 colors.

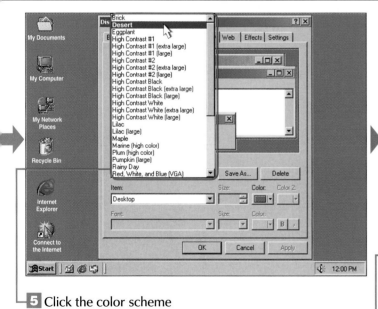

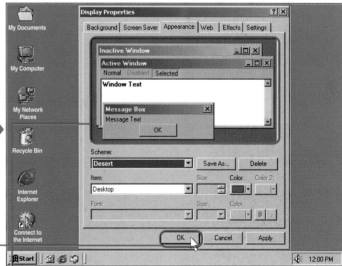

5 Click the color scheme you want to use.

■ This area displays how your screen will look with the color scheme you selected.

6 Click **OK** to change the color scheme.

■ To return to the original color scheme, perform steps 1 to 6, selecting **Windows Standard** in step 5.

You can change the amount of information that can fit on your screen.

Lower resolutions display larger images on the screen. This lets you see information more clearly.

Higher resolutions display smaller images on the screen. This lets you display more information on the screen at once.

CHANGE SCREEN RESOLUTION

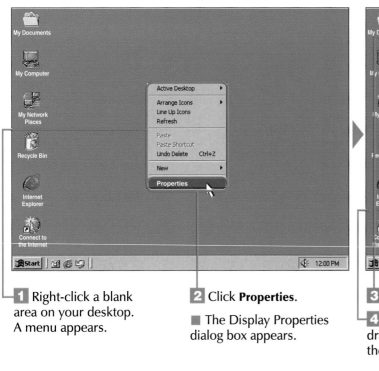

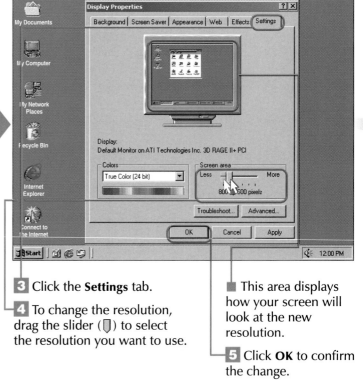

1 Right-click a blank area on your desktop. A menu appears.

2 Click **Properties**.

■ The Display Properties dialog box appears.

3 Click the **Settings** tab.

4 To change the resolution, drag the slider (⬜) to select the resolution you want to use.

■ This area displays how your screen will look at the new resolution.

5 Click **OK** to confirm the change.

What determines which screen resolutions are available on my computer?

Your monitor and video card determine which screen resolutions you can use.

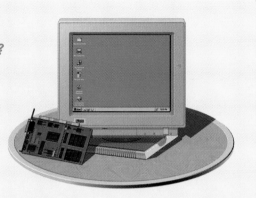

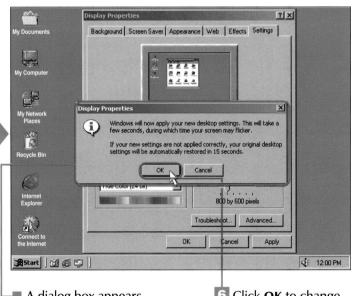

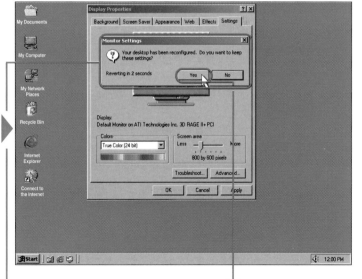

■ A dialog box appears, stating that Windows will take a few seconds to change the screen resolution. Your screen may flicker during this time.

6 Click **OK** to change the resolution.

■ Windows resizes the information on your screen.

■ The Monitor Settings dialog box appears, asking if you want to keep the new screen resolution.

7 Click **Yes** to keep the screen resolution.

CHANGE MOUSE SETTINGS

You can change the way your mouse works to suit your needs.

CHANGE MOUSE SETTINGS

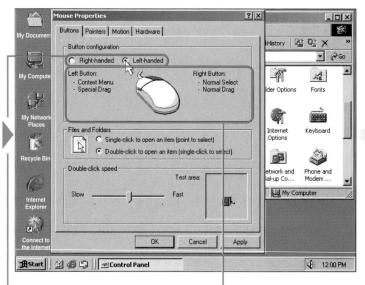

1 Click **Start**.

2 Click **Settings**.

3 Click **Control Panel**.

■ The Control Panel window appears.

4 Double-click **Mouse** to change the mouse settings.

■ The Mouse Properties dialog box appears.

SWITCH BUTTONS

5 To switch the functions of the left and right mouse buttons, click an option to specify if you are right-handed or left-handed (○ changes to ⊙).

■ This area describes the functions of the left and right mouse buttons, depending on the option you selected.

How can I use the mouse to open and select files and folders?

Single-click

This option is useful for people who have trouble double-clicking. To open an item, click the left mouse button once. To select an item, position the mouse pointer over the item.

Double-click

This option is useful for experienced mouse users. To open an item, quickly click the left mouse button twice. To select an item, click the left mouse button once.

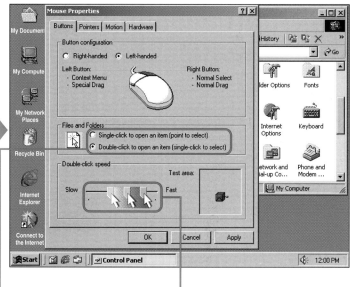

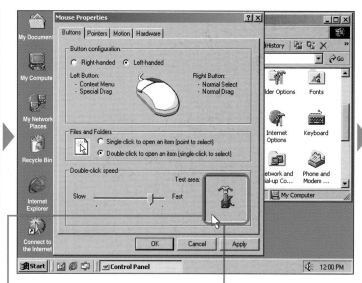

USE SINGLE-CLICK OR DOUBLE-CLICK

6 To specify if you want to open items using a single-click or a double-click, click an option (○ changes to ⊙).

DOUBLE-CLICK SPEED

7 To change the amount of time that can pass between two clicks of the mouse button for Windows to recognize a double-click, drag the slider (▯) to a new position.

8 Double-click this area to test the double-click speed.

■ The jack-in-the-box appears if you clicked at the correct speed.

CONTINUED ▶

You can personalize your mouse by changing the way the mouse pointer moves on your screen. You can also change the appearance of the mouse pointers Windows displays.

CHANGE MOUSE SETTINGS (CONTINUED)

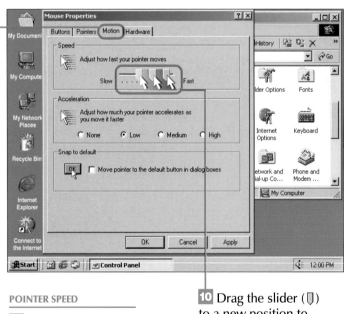

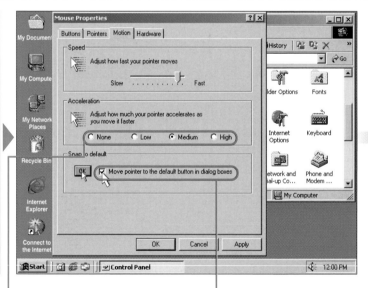

POINTER SPEED

9 To make the mouse pointer on your screen move faster or slower, click the **Motion** tab.

10 Drag the slider (🔲) to a new position to change the pointer speed.

POINTER ACCELERATION

11 To specify how fast the mouse pointer on your screen moves compared to how fast you move the mouse on your desk, click an option (○ changes to ⊙).

SNAP TO DEFAULT

12 To have the mouse pointer automatically appear over the default button in many dialog boxes, click this option (☐ changes to ☑).

Note: The default button in many dialog boxes is **OK**.

Should I use a mouse pad?

A mouse pad provides a smooth surface for moving the mouse on your desk. A mouse pad reduces the amount of dirt that enters the mouse and protects your desk from scratches. Hard plastic mouse pads attract less dirt and provide a smoother surface than fabric mouse pads.

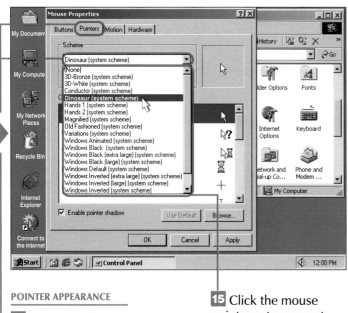

POINTER APPEARANCE

13 To change the appearance of the mouse pointers, click the **Pointers** tab.

14 Click this area to display a list of the mouse pointer sets.

15 Click the mouse pointer set you want to use.

■ This area displays the mouse pointers that make up the set you selected.

CONFIRM CHANGES

16 Click **OK** when you finish selecting all the mouse settings you want to change.

If you share your computer with one or more people, you can create a new user account so each person can use their own personalized settings.

You must be logged on to your computer as an administrator to create a new user account. See page 20 to log on to a computer.

CREATE A NEW USER ON YOUR COMPUTER

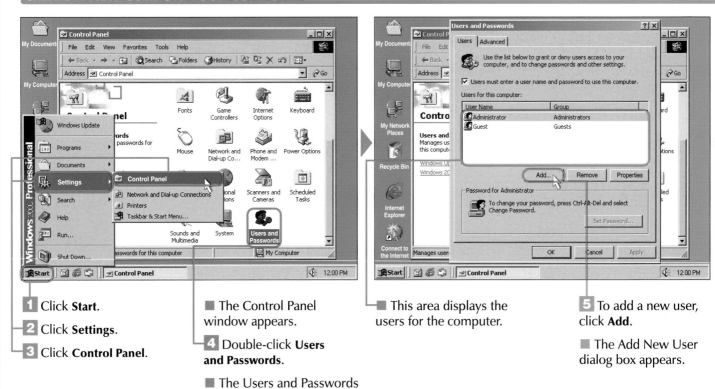

1 Click **Start**.

2 Click **Settings**.

3 Click **Control Panel**.

■ The Control Panel window appears.

4 Double-click **Users and Passwords**.

■ The Users and Passwords dialog box appears.

■ This area displays the users for the computer.

5 To add a new user, click **Add**.

■ The Add New User dialog box appears.

108

TIP

My computer is part of a network. Can I create a new user on the network?

If your computer is part of a network, you must see your network administrator for information on adding a new user.

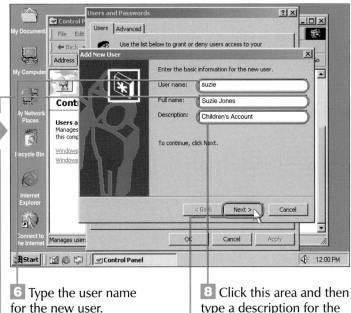

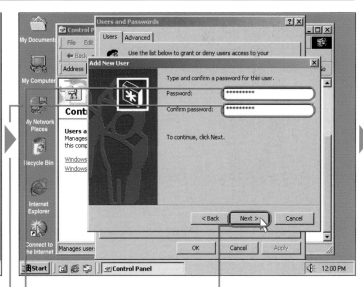

6 Type the user name for the new user.

7 Click this area and then type the full name of the new user.

8 Click this area and then type a description for the new user.

9 Click **Next** to continue.

10 Click this area and then type the password for the new user.

11 Click this area and then type the password again.

12 Click **Next** to continue.

CONTINUED

You can specify the type of access you want to grant a new user. The access you grant determines the type of tasks the user can perform on the computer.

STANDARD USER

Access
- ☑ Modify Computer
- ☑ Install Programs
- ☐ Read Other User Files

RESTRICTED USER

Access
- ☑ Save Documents
- ☐ Install Programs
- ☐ Change System Files

CREATE A NEW USER ON YOUR COMPUTER (CONTINUED)

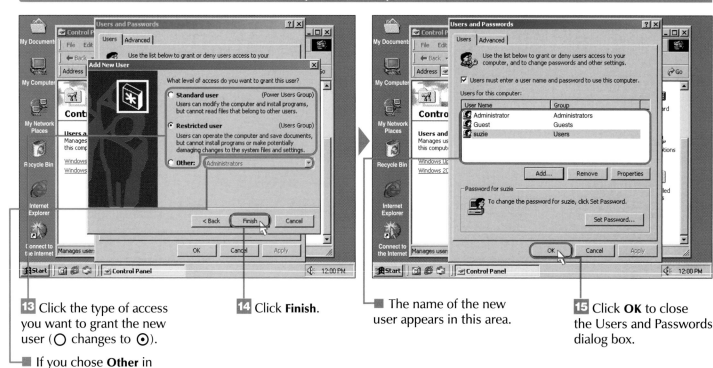

13 Click the type of access you want to grant the new user (○ changes to ⊙).

■ If you chose **Other** in step **13**, you can click this area to specify the type of access you want to grant.

14 Click **Finish**.

■ The name of the new user appears in this area.

15 Click **OK** to close the Users and Passwords dialog box.

You must be logged on to your computer as an administrator to delete a user account. See page 20 to log on to a computer.

DELETE A USER FROM YOUR COMPUTER

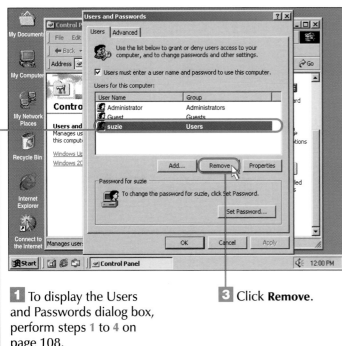

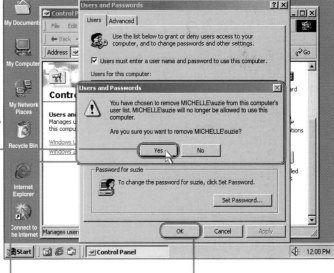

1 To display the Users and Passwords dialog box, perform steps **1** to **4** on page 108.

2 Click the user you want to remove.

3 Click **Remove**.

■ A confirmation dialog box appears.

4 Click **Yes** to remove the user from the computer.

■ The user is removed from the users list.

5 Click **OK** to close the Users and Passwords dialog box.

CHAPTER 7

HAVE FUN WITH WINDOWS

Ready to have some fun? Read this chapter to learn how to play games and listen to music CDs on your computer.

Windows includes several games you can play on your computer. Games are a fun way to improve your mouse skills and hand-eye coordination.

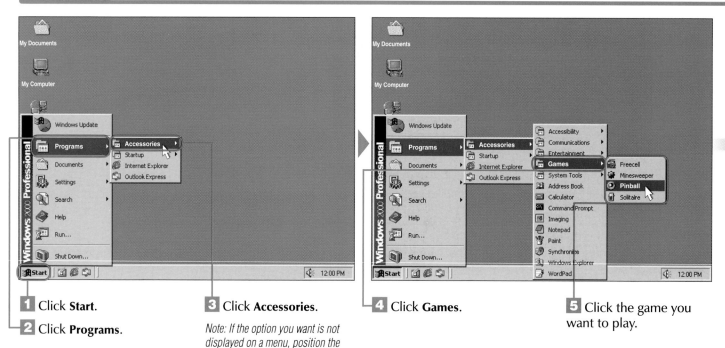

1 Click **Start**.

2 Click **Programs**.

3 Click **Accessories**.

Note: If the option you want is not displayed on a menu, position the mouse ▷ over the bottom of the menu to display all the options.

4 Click **Games**.

5 Click the game you want to play.

What other games are included with Windows?

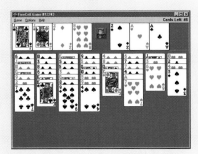

FreeCell

FreeCell is a single-player card game.

Minesweeper

Minesweeper is a strategy game in which you try to avoid being blown up by mines.

PINBALL

Pinball is similar to a pinball game you would find at an arcade. You launch a ball and then try to score as many points as possible.

SOLITAIRE

Solitaire is a classic card game that you play on your own. You try to put all the cards in order from ace to king in four stacks, one stack for each suit.

You can use your computer to play music CDs while you work.

You need a CD-ROM drive, a sound card and speakers to play music CDs.

PLAY A MUSIC CD

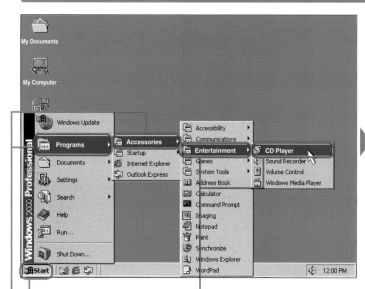

1 Click **Start**.

2 Click **Programs**.

3 Click **Accessories**.

Note: If the option you want is not displayed on a menu, position the mouse ▷ over the bottom of the menu to display all the options.

4 Click **Entertainment**.

5 Click **CD Player**.

■ The CD Player window appears.

6 Insert a music CD into the CD-ROM drive.

■ A dialog box may appear, asking if you want to download information about the CD from the Internet, such as the name of the artist and each song.

7 To have CD Player download information about the CD, click **OK**.

Note: If you are not connected to the Internet, a dialog box appears that allows you to connect.

Can I listen to music privately?

You can listen to music privately by plugging a headset into your CD-ROM drive.

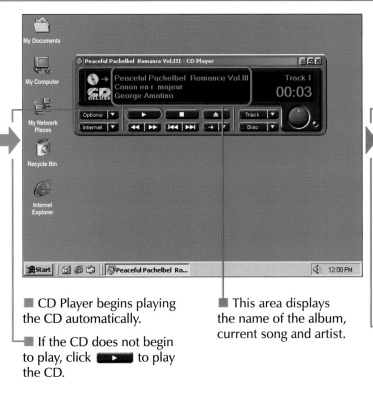

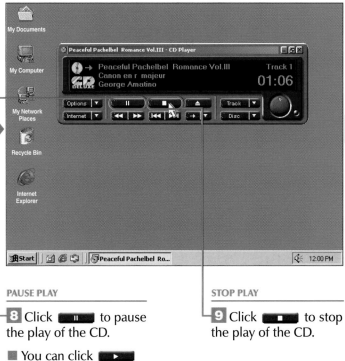

■ CD Player begins playing the CD automatically.

■ If the CD does not begin to play, click ▶ to play the CD.

■ This area displays the name of the album, current song and artist.

PAUSE PLAY

8 Click ❚❚ to pause the play of the CD.

■ You can click ▶ to resume the play.

STOP PLAY

9 Click ■ to stop the play of the CD.

CONTINUED ▶

PLAY A MUSIC CD (CONTINUED)

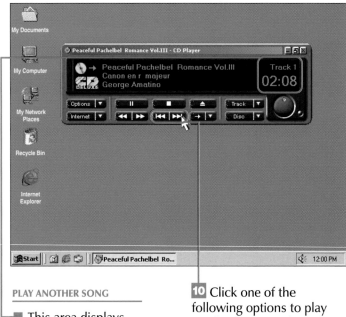

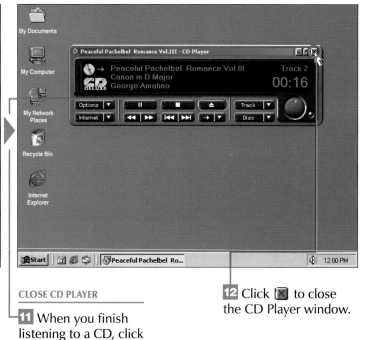

PLAY ANOTHER SONG

■ This area displays which song is currently playing and the amount of time the song has played.

10 Click one of the following options to play another song on the CD.

[◄◄] Play the previous song

[►►] Play the next song

CLOSE CD PLAYER

11 When you finish listening to a CD, click [▲] to eject the CD.

12 Click [X] to close the CD Player window.

You can easily adjust the volume of sound coming from your speakers.

Adjusting the volume will affect all the sounds you play on your computer, such as sound from a music CD or video.

ADJUST THE VOLUME

1 Click ◄€ to display the Volume control.

2 Drag the slider (☐) up or down to increase or decrease the volume.

3 Click this option to turn off the volume (☐ changes to ☑). The speaker icon (◄€) changes to ⊕ on the taskbar.

Note: You can repeat step 3 to once again turn on the volume.

■ To hide the Volume control, click outside the box.

ASSIGN SOUNDS TO PROGRAM EVENTS

You can have Windows play sound effects when you perform certain tasks on your computer.

For example, you can hear a phone ring when you receive a fax or music when you exit Windows.

ASSIGN A SOUND SCHEME

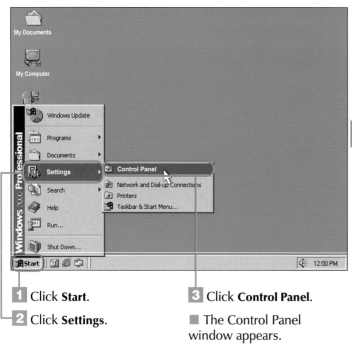

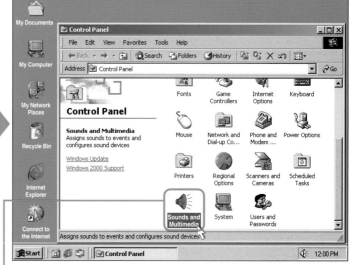

1 Click **Start**.

2 Click **Settings**.

3 Click **Control Panel**.

■ The Control Panel window appears.

4 Double-click **Sounds and Multimedia**.

■ The Sounds and Multimedia Properties dialog box appears.

What do I need to hear sounds on my computer?

You need a sound card and speakers on your computer to hear sounds. If your sound card and speakers are set up properly, you will hear a short musical introduction each time Windows starts.

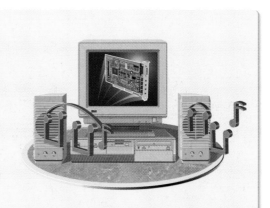

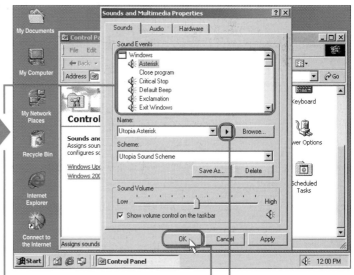

■ This area displays the events to which you can assign sounds.

5 Click this area to display a list of the available sound schemes. Each scheme will change the sounds for many events at once.

6 Click the scheme you want to use.

*Note: A dialog box may appear, asking if you want to save the previous scheme. Click **No** to continue without saving.*

■ A speaker icon (🔊) appears beside each event that will play a sound.

7 To hear the sound an event will play, click the event.

8 Click ▶ to hear the sound.

Note: To adjust the volume of the sound, see page 119.

9 Click **OK** to confirm your selection.

ASSIGN SOUNDS TO PROGRAM EVENTS

You can assign a sound to an event performed on your computer.

You may want to hear your favorite cartoon character each time you close a program or a sigh of relief when you restore a window.

ASSIGN A SOUND TO ONE EVENT

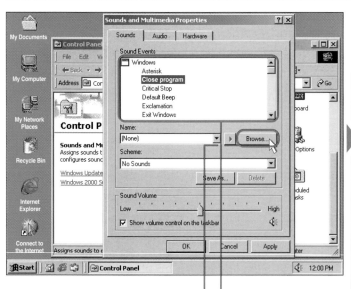

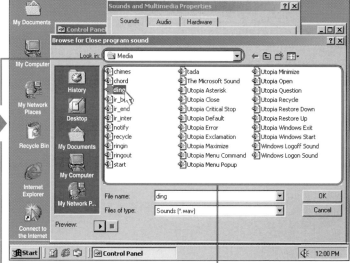

1 Display the Sounds and Multimedia Properties dialog box.

Note: To display the Sounds and Multimedia Properties dialog box, perform steps 1 to 4 on page 120.

2 Click the event to which you want to assign a sound.

3 Click **Browse** to find the sound you want to use on your computer.

■ The Browse dialog box appears.

■ This area shows the location of the displayed sound files. You can click this area to change the location.

4 Click the sound you want to hear every time the event occurs.

122

Where can I get more sounds?

You can purchase sounds at computer stores or get sounds on the Internet. Make sure you use sounds with the .wav extension, such as **wolfhowl.wav**.

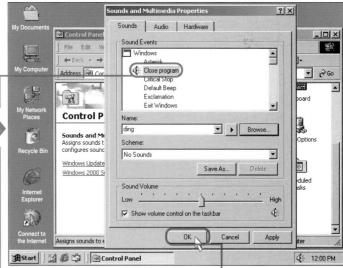

5 Click ► to play the sound you selected.

6 Click **OK** to select the sound.

■ A speaker icon (◄) appears beside the event.

7 To assign sounds to other events, repeat steps 2 to 6 for each event.

8 Click **OK** to confirm your changes.

CHAPTER 8

OPTIMIZE YOUR COMPUTER

Are you wondering how to get the most out of your computer? This chapter shows you how to keep your computer running efficiently by detecting and repairing disk errors, deleting unnecessary files and much more.

You must format a floppy disk before you can use the disk to store information.

Floppy disks you buy at computer stores are usually formatted. You may want to later format a disk to erase the information it contains and prepare the disk for storing new information.

FORMAT A FLOPPY DISK

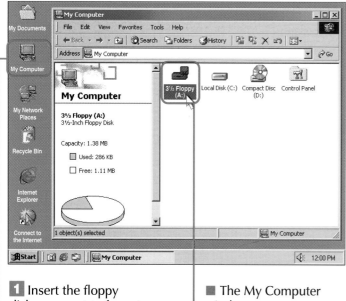

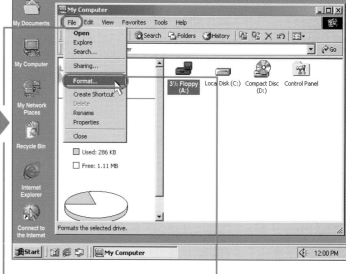

1 Insert the floppy disk you want to format into the floppy drive.

2 Double-click **My Computer**.

■ The My Computer window appears.

3 Click the drive containing the floppy disk you want to format (example: **A:**).

4 Click **File**.

5 Click **Format**.

■ The Format dialog box appears.

126

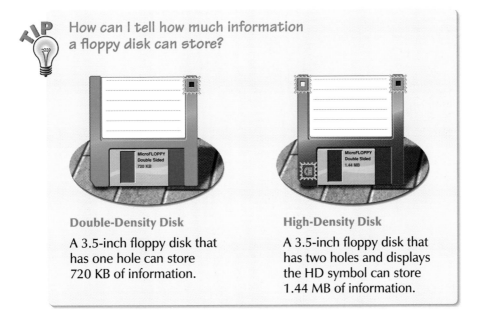

How can I tell how much information a floppy disk can store?

Double-Density Disk

A 3.5-inch floppy disk that has one hole can store 720 KB of information.

High-Density Disk

A 3.5-inch floppy disk that has two holes and displays the HD symbol can store 1.44 MB of information.

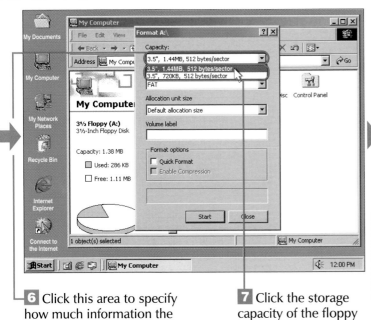

6 Click this area to specify how much information the floppy disk can store.

7 Click the storage capacity of the floppy disk.

8 Click **Start** to start formatting the floppy disk.

CONTINUED

Before formatting a floppy disk, make sure the disk does not contain information you may need. Formatting a floppy disk will permanently remove all the information on the disk.

FORMAT A FLOPPY DISK (CONTINUED)

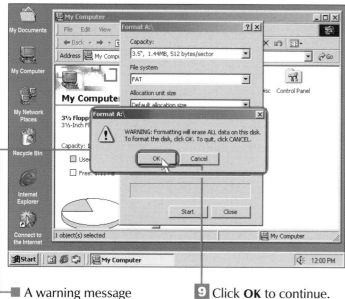

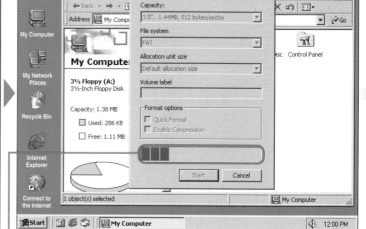

■ A warning message appears, indicating that formatting the floppy disk will erase all the data on the disk.

9 Click **OK** to continue.

■ This area displays the progress of the format.

128

How can I tell if a floppy disk is formatted?

Windows will display an error message when you try to view the contents of a disk that is not formatted. You cannot tell if a floppy disk is formatted just by looking at the disk.

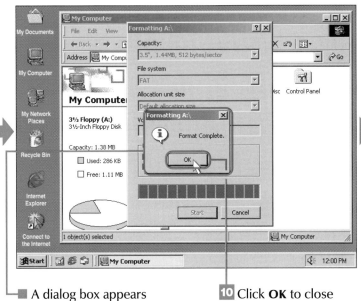

■ A dialog box appears when the format is complete.

10 Click **OK** to close the dialog box.

■ To format another floppy disk, insert the disk and then repeat steps **6** to **10** starting on page 127.

11 Click **Close** to close the Format dialog box.

You can improve the performance of your computer by checking for hard disk errors. Windows will attempt to automatically repair any disk errors it finds.

The hard disk is the primary device a computer uses to store information.

You must be logged on to your computer or network as an administrator to detect and repair disk errors. See page 20 to log on to a computer or network.

DETECT AND REPAIR DISK ERRORS

1 Double-click **My Computer**.

■ The My Computer window appears.

2 Click the disk you want to check for errors.

3 Click **File**.

4 Click **Properties**.

■ The Properties dialog box appears.

TIP

Can I work with files on my computer while Windows checks for disk errors?

You should not have any files open while Windows checks for disk errors. If you have files open, Windows may not be able to check the disk properly. Open files may also increase the time it takes for Windows to complete the check.

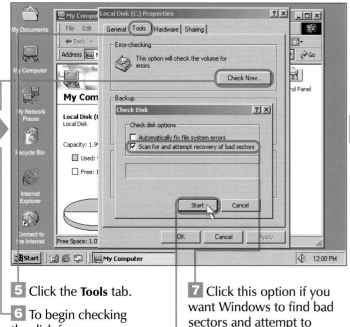

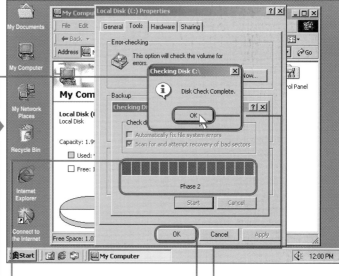

5 Click the **Tools** tab.

6 To begin checking the disk for errors, click **Check Now**.

■ The Check Disk dialog box appears.

7 Click this option if you want Windows to find bad sectors and attempt to recover information from the sectors (☐ changes to ☑).

8 Click **Start** to start the check.

■ This area displays the progress of the check.

■ A dialog box appears when the check is complete.

9 Click **OK** to close the dialog box.

10 Click **OK** to close the Properties dialog box.

You can improve the performance of your computer by defragmenting your hard disk.

You must be logged on to your computer or network as an administrator to defragment a hard disk. See page 20 to log on to a computer or network.

DEFRAGMENT YOUR HARD DISK

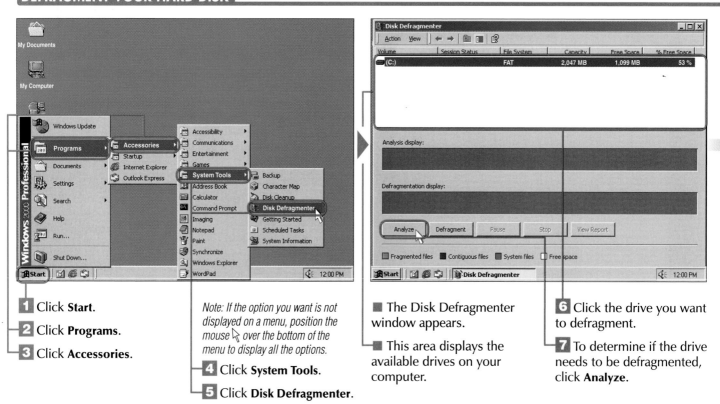

1 Click **Start**.

2 Click **Programs**.

3 Click **Accessories**.

Note: If the option you want is not displayed on a menu, position the mouse ₖ over the bottom of the menu to display all the options.

4 Click **System Tools**.

5 Click **Disk Defragmenter**.

■ The Disk Defragmenter window appears.

■ This area displays the available drives on your computer.

6 Click the drive you want to defragment.

7 To determine if the drive needs to be defragmented, click **Analyze**.

Why would I need to defragment my hard disk?

A fragmented hard disk stores parts of a file in many different locations. Your computer must search many areas on the disk to retrieve a file. You can use Disk Defragmenter to place all the parts of a file in one location. This reduces the time your computer will spend locating the file.

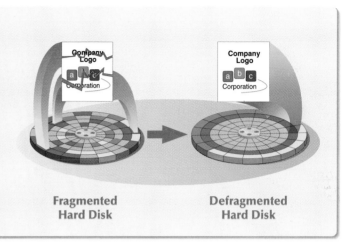

Fragmented
Hard Disk

Defragmented
Hard Disk

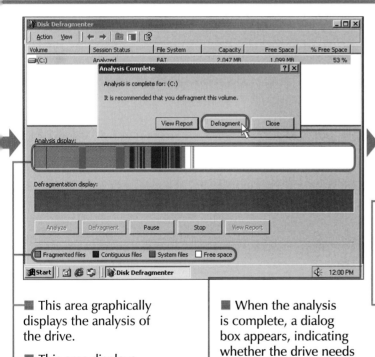

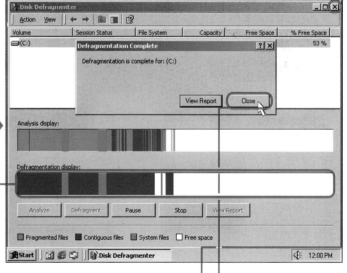

■ This area graphically displays the analysis of the drive.

■ This area displays a legend. The legend indicates what each color represents.

■ When the analysis is complete, a dialog box appears, indicating whether the drive needs to be defragmented.

8 To defragment the drive, click **Defragment**.

■ This area graphically displays the defragmentation process.

■ A dialog box appears when the defragmentation is complete.

9 Click **Close** to close the dialog box.

10 Click **X** to close the Disk Defragmenter window.

■ You can now use your computer as usual.

Disk Cleanup will remove unnecessary files from your computer to free up disk space.

USING DISK CLEANUP

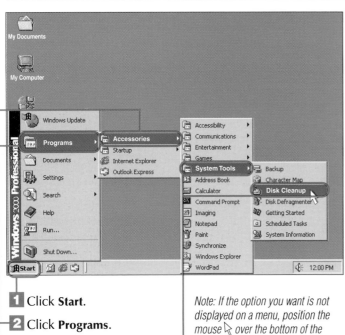

1 Click **Start**.

2 Click **Programs**.

3 Click **Accessories**.

Note: If the option you want is not displayed on a menu, position the mouse ▷ over the bottom of the menu to display all the options.

4 Click **System Tools**.

5 Click **Disk Cleanup**.

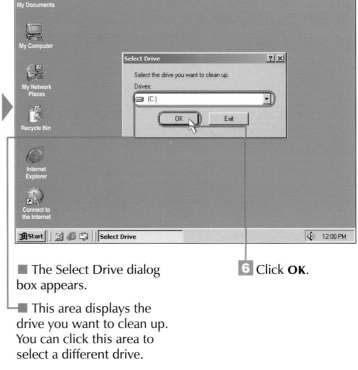

■ The Select Drive dialog box appears.

■ This area displays the drive you want to clean up. You can click this area to select a different drive.

6 Click **OK**.

TIP

What types of files can
Disk Cleanup remove?

Downloaded Program Files

Information transferred from the Internet when you view certain Web pages.

Temporary Internet Files

Web pages stored on your computer for quick viewing.

Recycle Bin

Files you have deleted.

Offline Files

Copies of files on the network you have made available offline.

Temporary Offline Files

Copies of files you have recently used on the network.

Catalog files for the Content Indexer

Files created to speed up searches on your computer.

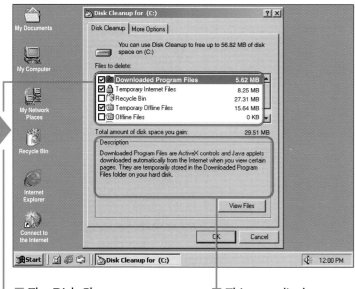

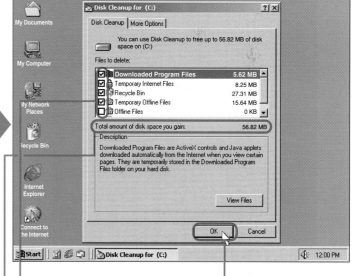

■ The Disk Cleanup dialog box appears.

■ This area displays the types of files you can remove and the amount of disk space taken up by each file type.

■ This area displays a description of the highlighted file type.

7 Windows will remove the files for each file type that displays a check mark (☑). You can click the box (☐) beside a file type to add or remove the check mark.

■ This area displays the total space Windows will free up from the file types you selected.

8 Click **OK** to remove the files.

■ A confirmation dialog box appears. Click **Yes** to permanently delete the files.

You can add a new program to your computer. Programs come on a CD-ROM disc or floppy disks.

You must be logged on to your computer as an administrator to install a program. See page 20 to log on to a computer.

INSTALL A PROGRAM

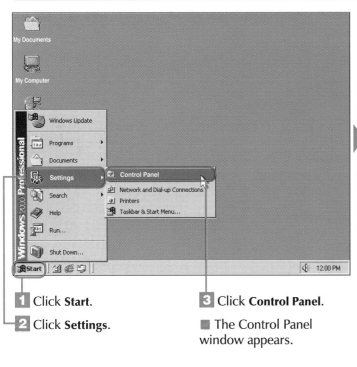

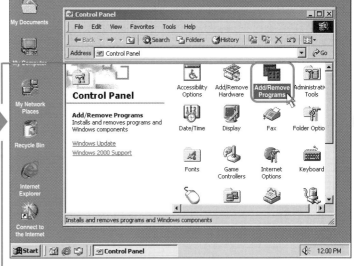

1 Click **Start**.

2 Click **Settings**.

3 Click **Control Panel**.

■ The Control Panel window appears.

4 Double-click **Add/Remove Programs**.

■ The Add/Remove Programs window appears.

Why did an installation program automatically start?

Most Windows programs available on a CD-ROM disc will automatically start an installation program when you insert the CD-ROM disc into the drive. Follow the instructions on your screen to install the program.

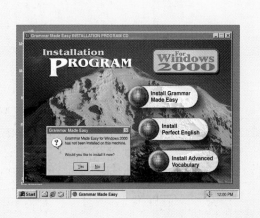

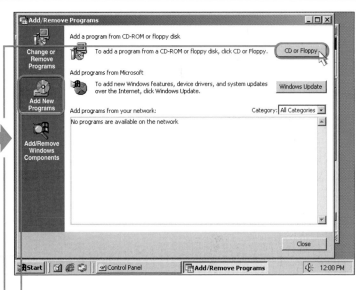

5 Click **Add New Programs** to install a new program.

6 To install a program from a CD-ROM disc or floppy disk, click **CD or Floppy**.

■ The Install Program From Floppy Disk or CD-ROM dialog box appears.

7 Insert the program's first installation floppy disk or CD-ROM disc into a drive.

8 Click **Next** to continue.

CONTINUED

There are three common ways to install a program.

Typical

Sets up the program with the most common components.

Custom

Lets you customize the program to suit your specific needs.

Minimum

Sets up the program with a minimum number of components. This is ideal for computers with limited disk space.

INSTALL A PROGRAM (CONTINUED)

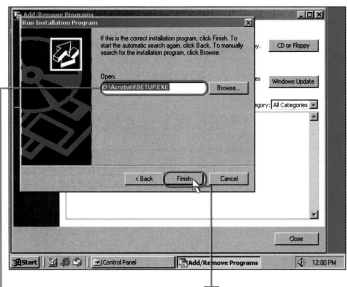

■ Windows locates the file needed to install the program.

9 Click **Finish** to install the program.

10 Follow the instructions on your screen. Every program will ask you a different set of questions.

■ After you install a program, make sure you keep the program's CD-ROM disc or floppy disks in a safe place. If your computer fails or you accidentally erase the program files, you may need to install the program again.

You can remove a program that you no longer use on your computer. Removing a program will free up space on your hard drive.

REMOVE A PROGRAM

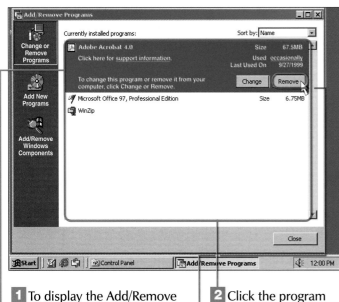

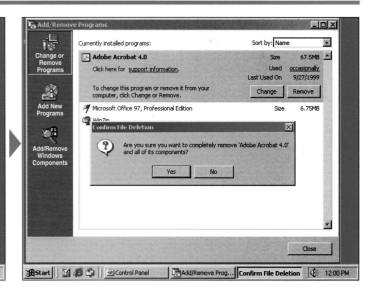

1 To display the Add/Remove Programs window, perform steps 1 to 4 on page 136.

■ This area lists the programs Windows can automatically remove.

2 Click the program you want to remove.

3 Click **Change/Remove** or **Remove**.

Note: The name of the button depends on the program you are removing.

4 Follow the instructions on your screen. Every program will take you through different steps to remove the program.

Before you can use a new printer, you need to install the printer on your computer.

You must be logged on to your computer or network as an administrator to install a printer. See page 20 to log on to a computer or network.

INSTALL A PRINTER

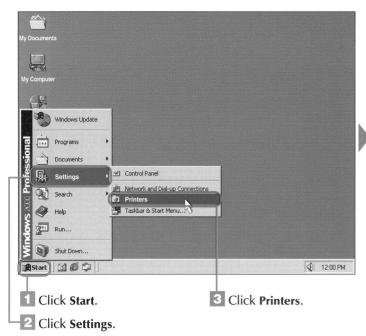

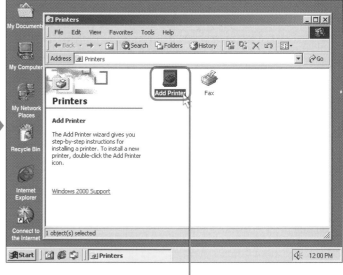

1 Click **Start**.

2 Click **Settings**.

3 Click **Printers**.

■ The Printers window appears.

4 Double-click **Add Printer** to install a new printer.

What is a Plug and Play printer?

A Plug and Play printer is a printer that Windows can automatically set up to work properly with your computer, which makes the printer easy to install. If your printer is Plug and Play, Windows may automatically install the printer for you the first time you turn on your computer after connecting the printer to the computer.

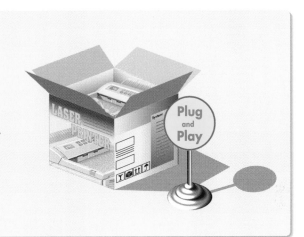

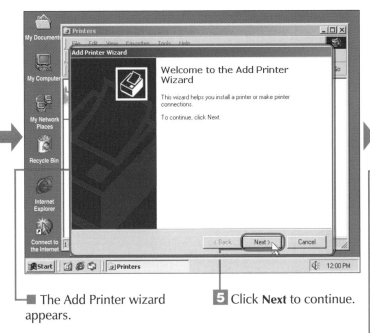

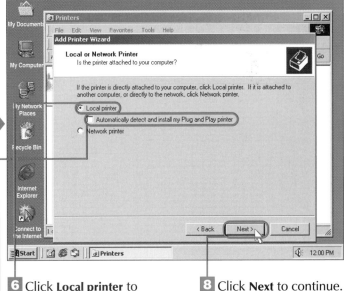

■ The Add Printer wizard appears.

5 Click **Next** to continue.

6 Click **Local printer** to install a printer that connects directly to your computer (○ changes to ⊙).

7 Click this option if your printer is not Plug and Play (☑ changes to ☐). The wizard will not attempt to detect and install the printer automatically.

8 Click **Next** to continue.

CONTINUED ▶

When installing a printer, you must specify which port the printer is connected to. A port is a socket at the back of a computer where you plug in a device.

INSTALL A PRINTER (CONTINUED)

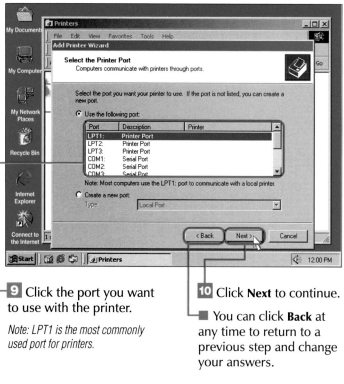

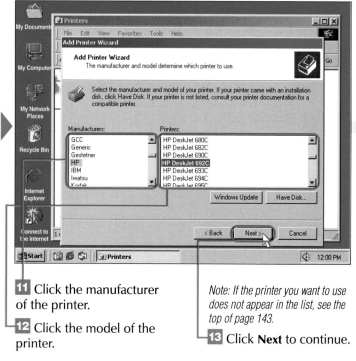

9 Click the port you want to use with the printer.

Note: LPT1 is the most commonly used port for printers.

10 Click **Next** to continue.

■ You can click **Back** at any time to return to a previous step and change your answers.

11 Click the manufacturer of the printer.

12 Click the model of the printer.

Note: If the printer you want to use does not appear in the list, see the top of page 143.

13 Click **Next** to continue.

What if the printer
I want to install
does not appear
in the list?

If the printer you want
to install does not
appear in the list, you
can use the installation
disk(s) that came with
the printer.

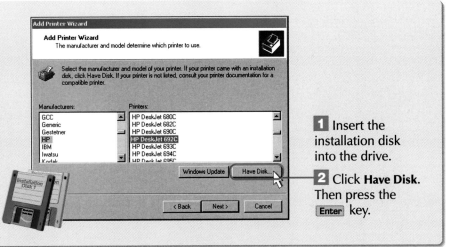

1 Insert the
installation disk
into the drive.

2 Click **Have Disk.**
Then press the
Enter key.

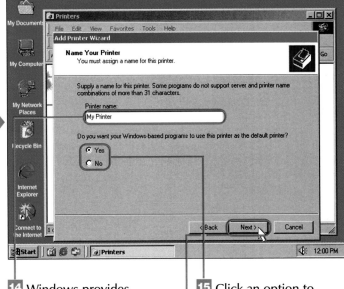

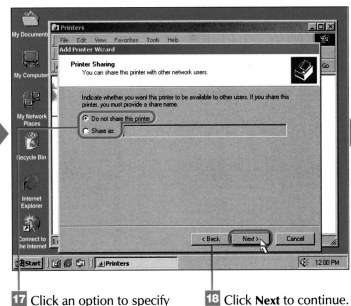

14 Windows provides
a name for the printer.
To use a different name,
type the name.

15 Click an option to
specify if you want to use
the printer as the default
printer (○ changes to ◉).
Files will automatically
print to the default printer.

16 Click **Next** to continue.

17 Click an option to specify
if you want to share the
printer with others on the
network (○ changes to ◉).

*Note: For information on sharing a
printer, see page 170.*

18 Click **Next** to continue.

CONTINUED

Windows allows you to print a test page to confirm that your printer is installed properly.

The test page contains information about the printer. You may want to keep the page for future reference.

INSTALL A PRINTER (CONTINUED)

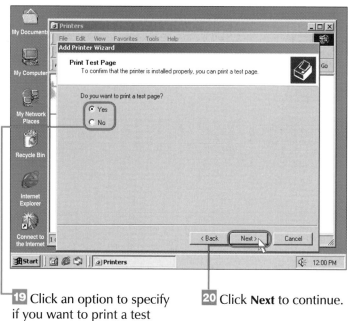

19 Click an option to specify if you want to print a test page (○ changes to ⊙).

20 Click **Next** to continue.

■ The wizard indicates that you have successfully completed the wizard.

21 Click **Finish** to install the printer.

Can I delete a printer?

If you no longer use a printer, you can delete the printer and disconnect the printer from your computer. You can delete a printer from the Printers window as you would delete a file on your computer. For information on deleting a file, see page 78.

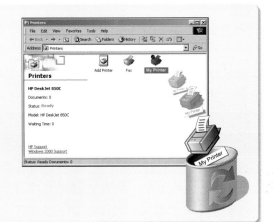

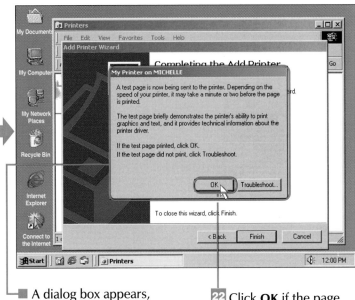

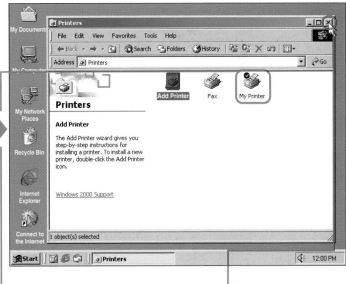

■ A dialog box appears, asking if the test page printed correctly.

*Note: This dialog box does not appear if you selected **No** in step 19.*

22 Click **OK** if the page printed correctly.

■ An icon for the printer appears in the Printers window.

■ The printer displays a check mark (✓) if you chose to make the printer the default printer in step 15.

23 Click ✕ to close the Printers window.

You can have Windows detect and install new hardware for you. You can add hardware such as a modem, mouse or keyboard.

You must be logged on to your computer or network as an administrator to install new hardware. See page 20 to log on to a computer or network.

INSTALL NEW HARDWARE

1 Click **Start**.

2 Click **Settings**.

3 Click **Control Panel**.

■ The Control Panel window appears.

4 Double-click **Add/Remove Hardware**.

■ The Add/Remove Hardware wizard appears.

5 Click **Next** to begin installing the new hardware.

Note: The steps you follow in the wizard may depend on the type of hardware device you are installing.

What are Plug and Play devices?

Plug and Play devices are devices that Windows can automatically set up to work properly with your computer, which makes them easy to install. Windows may automatically install a Plug and Play device for you the first time you turn on your computer after connecting the device to the computer.

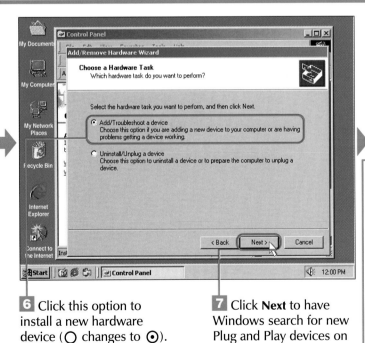

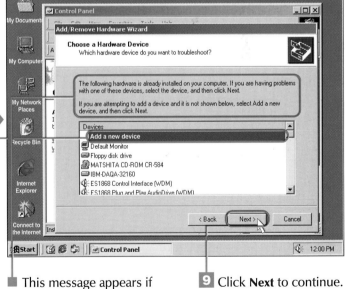

6 Click this option to install a new hardware device (○ changes to ⊙).

7 Click **Next** to have Windows search for new Plug and Play devices on your computer.

■ This message appears if Windows did not find any new Plug and Play devices.

8 Click **Add a new device** to install new hardware.

9 Click **Next** to continue.

CONTINUED

INSTALL NEW HARDWARE (CONTINUED)

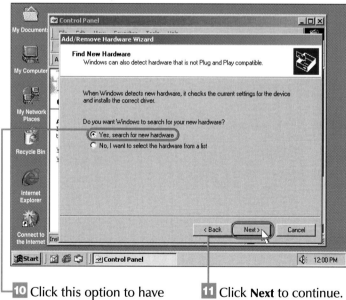

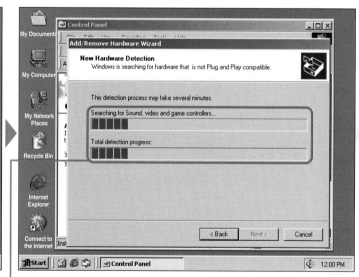

10 Click this option to have Windows search for new devices on your computer that are not Plug and Play (○ changes to ⊙).

11 Click **Next** to continue.

■ Windows searches for devices that are not Plug and Play.

■ This area displays the progress of the search. The search may take several minutes.

*Note: You can click **Cancel** to stop the search at any time.*

Why didn't my hardware device install properly?

The device you installed may not work properly with Windows 2000. To ensure your new hardware device will work with Windows 2000, check the documentation that came with the device or check Microsoft's Hardware Compatibility List. You can find the Hardware Compatibility List on the World Wide Web at:

www.microsoft.com/hcl

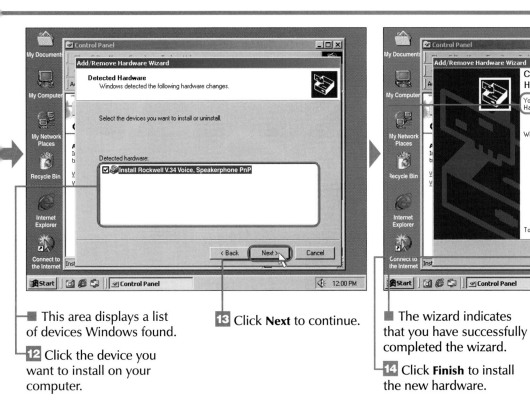

■ This area displays a list of devices Windows found.

12 Click the device you want to install on your computer.

13 Click **Next** to continue.

■ The wizard indicates that you have successfully completed the wizard.

14 Click **Finish** to install the new hardware.

■ You may be asked to insert the Windows CD-ROM disc or the floppy disk that came with the hardware.

■ You can now use your new hardware.

CHAPTER 9

WORK WITH FAXES

Would you like to use your computer to
send and receive faxes? Find out how in
this chapter.

You can easily send a fax to a colleague across the city or around the world.

You can use the Send Fax wizard to fax a message on a cover page.

You must have a fax modem installed on your computer to send and receive faxes.

SEND A FAX

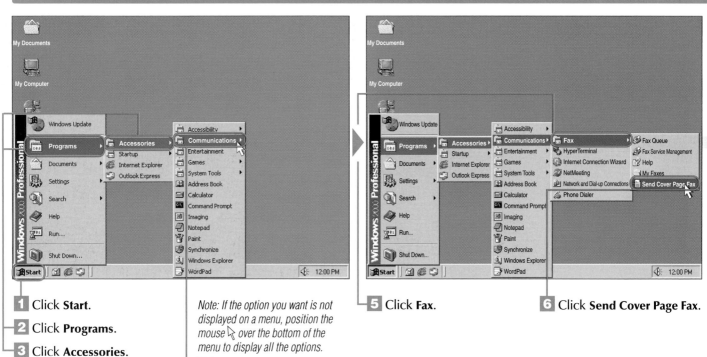

1 Click **Start**.

2 Click **Programs**.

3 Click **Accessories**.

Note: If the option you want is not displayed on a menu, position the mouse �)over the bottom of the menu to display all the options.

4 Click **Communications**.

5 Click **Fax**.

6 Click **Send Cover Page Fax**.

TIP

How can I fax a document I created on my computer?

Most programs allow you to use the program's Print feature to fax a document. For example, if you create a document in Microsoft Word, you can use Word's Print feature to fax the document.

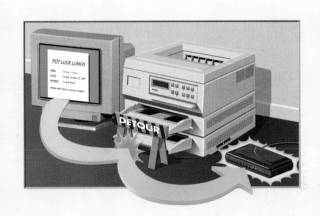

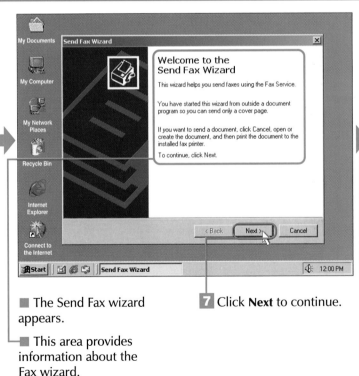

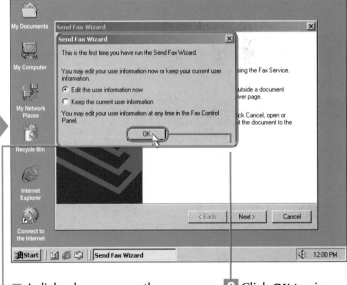

■ The Send Fax wizard appears.

■ This area provides information about the Fax wizard.

7 Click **Next** to continue.

■ A dialog box appears the first time you use the Send Fax wizard, asking if you want to change your user information.

8 Click **OK** to view and change your user information.

CONTINUED ▶

The first time you use the Send Fax wizard, you must update your user information. Windows will display your user information on the cover page of faxes you send.

USER INFORMATION

Your full name:
Fax number:
E-mail address:
Title:
Office location:
Home phone:
Address:
Billing code:
Company:
Department:
Work phone:

56K Fax Modem

SEND A FAX (CONTINUED)

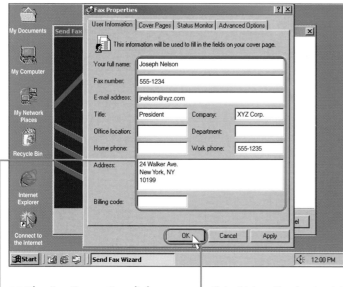

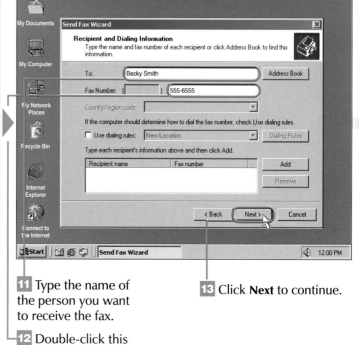

■ The Fax Properties dialog box appears.

9 Click each area where you want to enter information and then type the appropriate information.

Note: If information already exists in an area, drag the mouse I over the information and then press the **Delete** *key to remove the information.*

10 Click **OK** to confirm your changes.

11 Type the name of the person you want to receive the fax.

12 Double-click this area and then type the fax number.

13 Click **Next** to continue.

What types of cover pages can I select?

Windows offers four different cover pages you can select.

Confident

FYI

Generic

Urgent

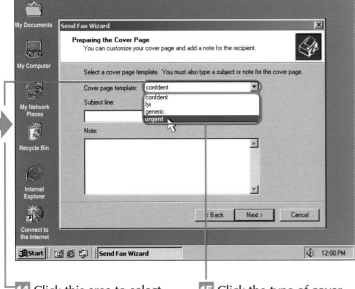

14 Click this area to select the type of cover page you want to use.

15 Click the type of cover page you want to use.

16 Click this area and type a subject for the fax.

17 Click this area and type a note you want to include with the fax.

18 Click **Next** to continue.

■ You can click **Back** at any time to return to a previous step and change your answers.

CONTINUED

You can choose when you want to send your fax. You can send the fax immediately, when long-distance rates are lower or at a time you specify.

If you delay sending a fax, make sure your computer is turned on when the fax will be sent.

SEND A FAX (CONTINUED)

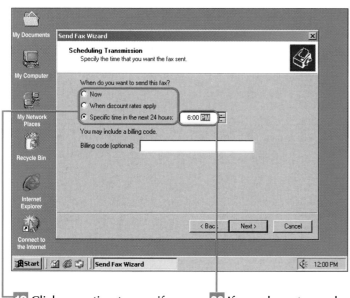

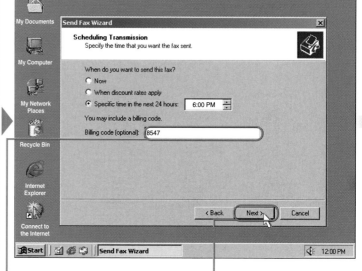

19 Click an option to specify when you want to send the fax (○ changes to ⊙).

20 If you chose to send the fax at a specific time, click each part of the time you want to change. Then type the correct information.

21 To include a billing code, click this area and type the code.

22 Click **Next** to continue.

TIP

Why would I include a billing code with a fax I send?

A billing code helps you keep track of the faxes you send and allows you to assign the costs to a specific account. This is useful if you frequently send faxes.

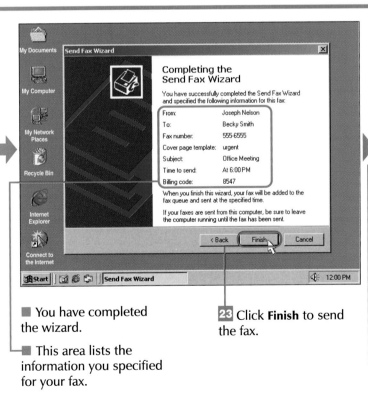

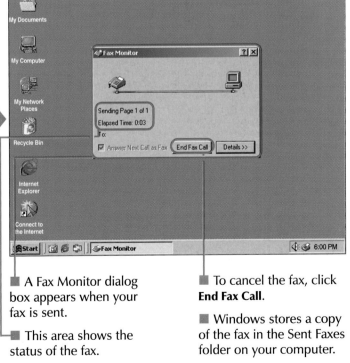

■ You have completed the wizard.

■ This area lists the information you specified for your fax.

23 Click **Finish** to send the fax.

■ A Fax Monitor dialog box appears when your fax is sent.

■ This area shows the status of the fax.

■ To cancel the fax, click **End Fax Call**.

■ Windows stores a copy of the fax in the Sent Faxes folder on your computer.

Before you can receive faxes on your computer, you must set up your fax modem.

You must be logged on to your computer or network as an administrator to set a fax modem to receive faxes. See page 20 to log on to a computer or network.

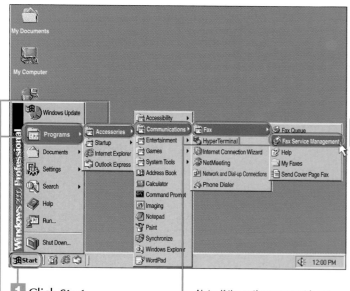

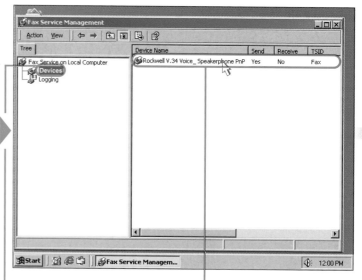

■1 Click **Start**.

■2 Click **Programs**.

■3 Click **Accessories**.

Note: If the option you want is not displayed on a menu, position the mouse ⌕ over the bottom of the menu to display all the options.

■4 Click **Communications**.

■5 Click **Fax**.

■6 Click **Fax Service Management**.

■ The Fax Service Management window appears.

■7 Click **Devices**.

■8 Double-click the fax modem to view the properties for the modem.

How will I know when I receive a fax?

Your fax modem will automatically answer the fax and the fax will transfer to your computer. The Fax Monitor icon () will appear at the bottom right corner of your screen to indicate that you received a fax. To view a fax, see page 160.

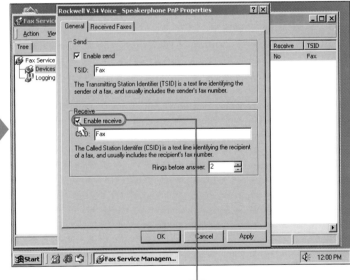

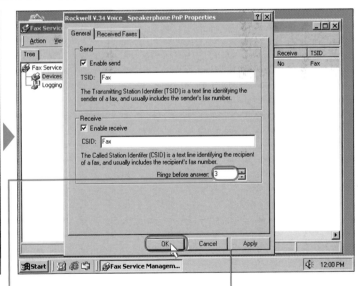

■ A dialog box appears.

9 To set up your fax modem to receive faxes, click this option (☐ changes to ☑).

10 To change the number of rings before the fax modem will answer a fax, double-click this area and type a new number.

11 Click **OK** to confirm your changes.

You can display faxes you have sent and faxes you have received.

VIEW FAXES

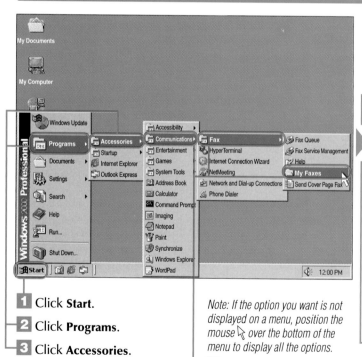

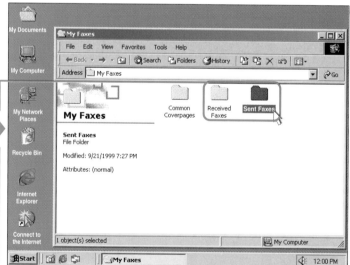

1 Click **Start**.

2 Click **Programs**.

3 Click **Accessories**.

Note: If the option you want is not displayed on a menu, position the mouse ⌖ over the bottom of the menu to display all the options.

4 Click **Communications**.

5 Click **Fax**.

6 Click **My Faxes**.

■ The My Faxes window appears.

7 Double-click the folder that contains the faxes you want to view.

Note: The Received Faxes folder stores faxes you have received. The Sent Faxes folder stores faxes you have sent.

TIP

A fax I received appears upside down. How can I view the fax properly?

You can rotate a fax to change the way it appears on your screen.

1 Click one of the following options to rotate the fax.

⊞ Rotate Left

⊞ Rotate Right

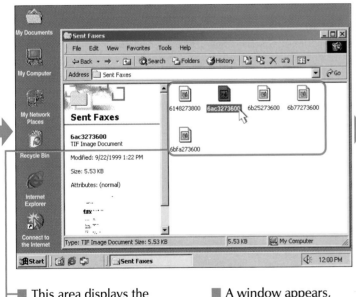

■ This area displays the faxes you have received or sent.

8 Double-click the fax you want to view.

■ A window appears, displaying the first page of the fax.

■ This area indicates which page you are viewing and the total number of pages in the fax.

9 Click one of these buttons to view the previous page (⊞) or the next page (⊞).

10 Click one of these buttons to magnify (🔍) or reduce (🔍) the page.

11 When you finish viewing the fax, click ✕ to close the window.

CHAPTER 10

WORK ON A NETWORK

Do you want to share information and equipment with other computers on a network? Learn how in this chapter.

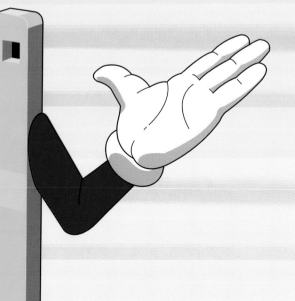

You can specify what information on your computer you want to share with individuals on a network.

Sharing information is useful if you and your colleagues are working together on a project and need to access the same files.

You must be logged on to your computer or network as an administrator to share a folder. See page 20 to log on to a computer or network.

SHARE A FOLDER

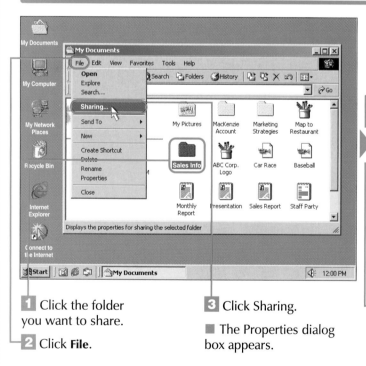

1 Click the folder you want to share.

2 Click **File**.

3 Click Sharing.

■ The Properties dialog box appears.

4 Click **Share this folder** to share the folder with others on the network (○ changes to ◉).

5 This area displays the name of the folder individuals will see on the network. To change the name, drag the mouse Ⅰ over the text until the text is highlighted. Then type a new name.

How can I access folders shared by other people on the network?

You can use My Network Places to see a list of the folders shared by your computer and other computers on the network. See page 176 to use My Network Places.

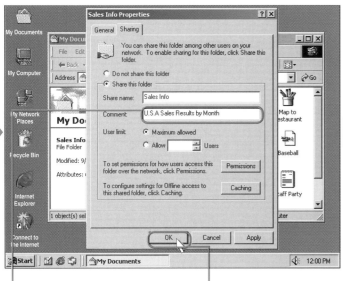

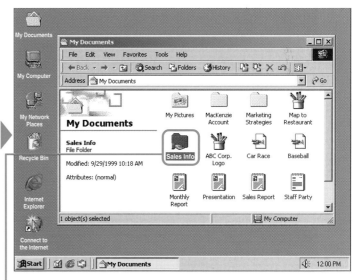

6 To enter a comment about the folder that individuals can see on the network, click this area and then type a comment.

7 Click **OK** to confirm your changes.

■ A hand (🖐) appears under the icon for the shared folder. Individuals on the network will have access to all the folders and files within the shared folder.

Note: To specify how people on the network can access the folder, see page 166.

■ To stop sharing a folder, repeat steps **1** to **4**, selecting **Do not share this folder** in step **4**. Then perform step **7**.

You can grant people, computers and groups on the network different types of access to a shared folder on your computer.

By default, everyone on the network has Full Control access to a shared folder on your computer.

You must be logged on to your computer or network as an administrator to change permissions for a shared folder. See page 20 to log on to a computer or network.

CHANGE PERMISSIONS FOR A SHARED FOLDER

■ Before you can change the permissions for a folder, you must share the folder. To share a folder, see page 164.

1 Click the folder you want to change the permissions for.

2 Click **File**.

3 Click **Sharing**.

■ The Properties dialog box appears.

4 Click **Permissions** to specify how people can access the folder over the network.

What types of access can I allow or deny for a shared folder on my computer?

Full Control

Users can open, change, create, move and delete files in the folder. Users may also be able to administer files.

Change

Users can open, change, create, move and delete files in the folder.

Read

Users can open but not change files in the folder.

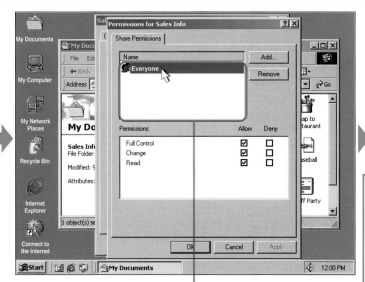

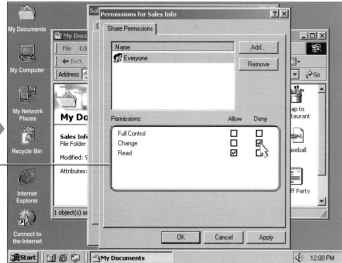

■ The Permissions dialog box appears.

■ This area lists each person, computer and group that can access the folder.

5 Click a person, computer or group to view their permissions.

■ This area displays the permissions granted to the person, computer or group. You can allow or deny permissions for Full Control, Change and Read access.

6 Click an option to allow or deny the permission.

Note: If more than one person, computer or group appears in the list, repeat steps 5 and 6 for each person, computer or group.

CONTINUED

CHANGE PERMISSIONS FOR A SHARED FOLDER (CONTINUED)

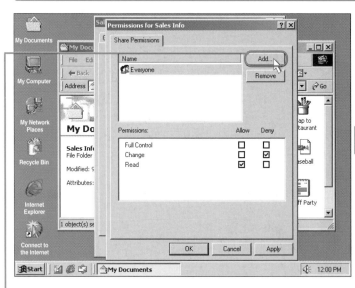

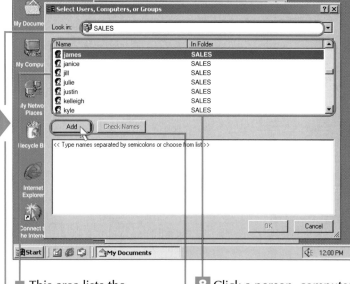

ADD A PERSON, COMPUTER OR GROUP

7 To add a person, computer or group to the list, click **Add**.

■ The Select Users, Computers, or Groups dialog box appears.

■ This area lists the people, computers and groups you can grant access to the folder.

■ This area displays the domain the people, computers and groups in the list belong to.

8 Click a person, computer or group you want to have access to the folder.

9 Click **Add** to add the person, computer or group.

How can I remove a person, computer or group from the Permissions dialog box?

If you no longer want a person, computer or group listed in the Permissions dialog box, click the person, computer or group you want to remove. Then press the `Delete` key.

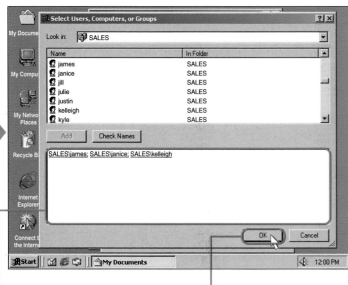

■ The person, computer or group you selected appears in this area.

10 Repeat steps **8** and **9** for each person, computer or group you want to have access to the folder.

11 Click **OK** to confirm your selections.

■ The people, computers and groups you selected appear in this area.

■ To assign permissions to a person, computer or group, perform steps **5** and **6** on page 167.

12 Click **OK** to confirm your changes.

*Note: If you chose to deny permission in step **6**, a confirmation dialog box may appear. Click **Yes** to close the dialog box.*

You can share your printer with other individuals on a network. This allows others to use your printer to print documents.

You can only share a printer that is directly connected to your computer.

You must be logged on to your computer or network as an administrator to share a printer. See page 20 to log on to a computer or network.

SHARE A PRINTER

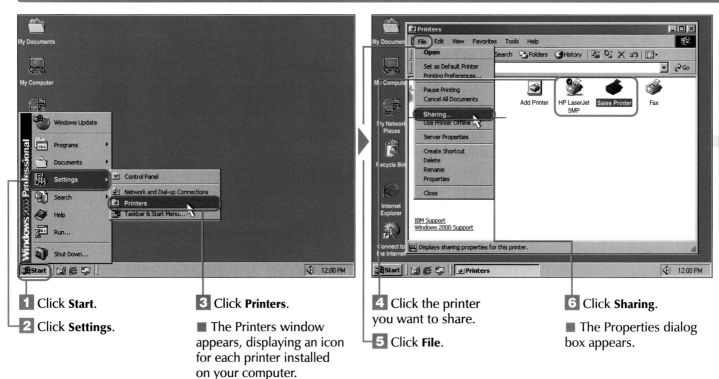

1 Click **Start**.

2 Click **Settings**.

3 Click **Printers**.

■ The Printers window appears, displaying an icon for each printer installed on your computer.

4 Click the printer you want to share.

5 Click **File**.

6 Click **Sharing**.

■ The Properties dialog box appears.

TIP

Will sharing a printer affect my computer's performance?

When individuals on the network send files to your printer, your computer temporarily stores the files before sending them to the printer. As a result, your computer will operate more slowly while other people use your printer.

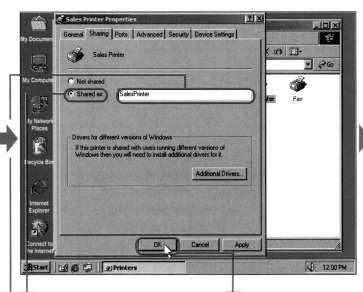

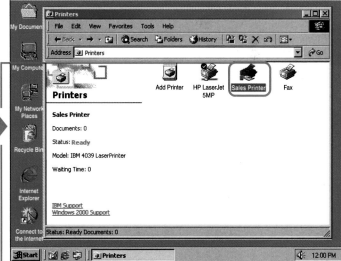

7 Click **Shared as** to share the printer with other people on the network (○ changes to ⊙).

■ This area displays the name of the printer people will see on the network. To change the name, type a new name.

8 Click **OK**.

*Note: A dialog box appears if you typed a printer name that contains spaces or more than 12 characters. Click **Yes** to use the printer name.*

■ A hand (🖐) appears under the icon for the printer you have shared, indicating that the printer is available to others on the network.

Note: To specify the type of access people have to the printer, see page 172.

■ To stop sharing a printer, repeat steps 1 to 8, selecting **Not shared** in step 7.

You can grant people, computers and groups on the network different types of access to a printer you have shared.

By default, everyone on the network has permission to print documents on the shared printer.

You must be logged on to your computer or network as an administrator to change permissions for a shared printer. See page 20 to log on to a computer or network.

CHANGE PERMISSIONS FOR A SHARED PRINTER

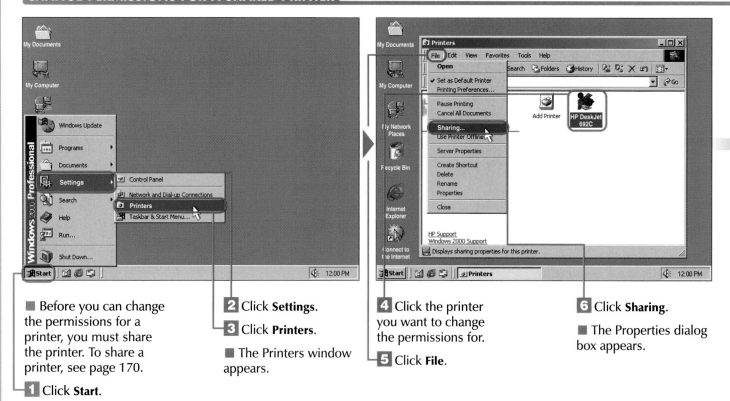

■ Before you can change the permissions for a printer, you must share the printer. To share a printer, see page 170.

1 Click **Start**.

2 Click **Settings**.

3 Click **Printers**.

■ The Printers window appears.

4 Click the printer you want to change the permissions for.

5 Click **File**.

6 Click **Sharing**.

■ The Properties dialog box appears.

What types of permissions can I allow or deny for a shared printer?

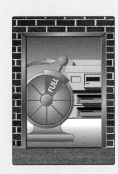

Print

Users can print and manage their own documents.

Manage Printers

Users have full control over the printer.

Manage Documents

Users can manage all documents waiting to print.

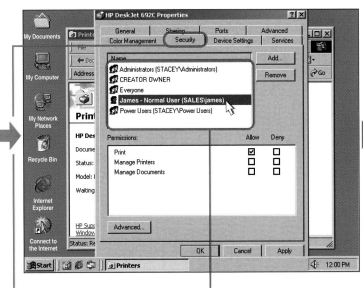

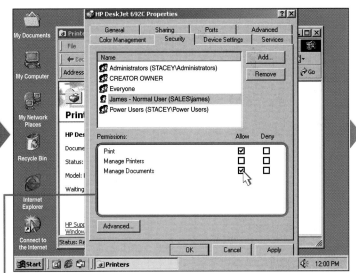

7 Click the **Security** tab.

■ This area lists each person, computer and group that can access the printer.

8 Click a person, computer or group to view their permissions.

■ This area displays the permissions granted to the person, computer or group. You can allow or deny permissions for Print, Manage Printers or Manage Documents.

9 Click an option to allow or deny the permission.

Note: If more than one person, computer or group appears in the list, repeat steps 8 and 9 for each person, computer or group.

CONTINUED

You can select which people, computers and groups on the network you want to have access to your shared printer.

CHANGE PERMISSIONS FOR A SHARED PRINTER (CONTINUED)

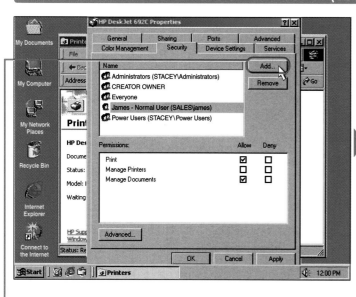

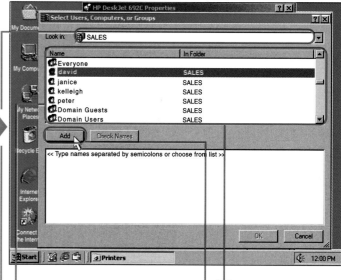

ADD A PERSON, COMPUTER OR GROUP

10 To add a person, computer or group to the list, click **Add**.

■ The Select Users, Computers, or Groups dialog box appears.

■ This area lists the people, computers and groups you can grant access to the printer.

■ This area displays the domain the people, computers and groups in the list belong to.

11 Click a person, computer or group you want to have access to the printer.

12 Click **Add** to add the person, computer or group.

TIP

What groups can I
allow or deny access
to a shared printer?

Windows allows you
to grant access to
many groups on your
computer or network.

Everyone

Every user is a member
of this group.

Domain Guests

Users who can perform
common tasks but do
not have their own user
name and password.

Domain Users

Users who can perform
common tasks.

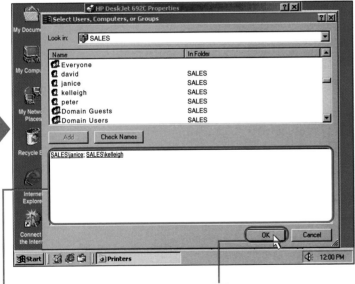

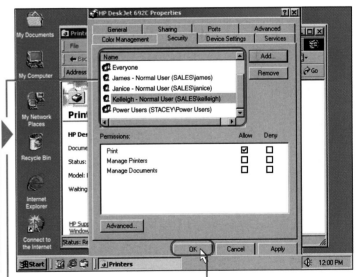

■ The person, computer or
group you selected appears
in this area.

13 Repeat steps **11** and **12**
for each person, computer
or group you want to have
access to the printer.

14 Click **OK** to confirm
your selections.

■ The people, computers
and groups you selected
appear in this area.

■ To assign permissions
to a person, computer or
group, perform steps **8**
and **9** on page 173.

15 Click **OK** to confirm
your changes.

*Note: If you chose to deny permission
in step 9, a confirmation dialog box
may appear. Click Yes to close the
dialog box.*

You can easily browse through the resources, such as files and printers, available on your network.

BROWSE THROUGH A NETWORK

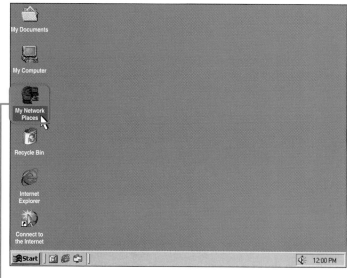

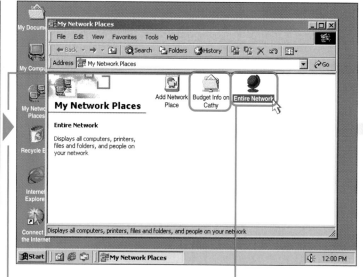

1 Double-click **My Network Places**.

■ The My Network Places window appears.

■ If you have previously worked with files in a shared folder on the network, the shared folder appears in the window. You can double-click the folder to quickly access the contents of the folder.

2 Double-click **Entire Network** to view all the computers and printers on your network.

TIP

What do the symbols in the My Network Places window represent?

Each item in the My Network Places window displays a symbol, or icon, to help you distinguish between the different types of items.

| Network operating system | Domain | Computer | Folder | Printer |

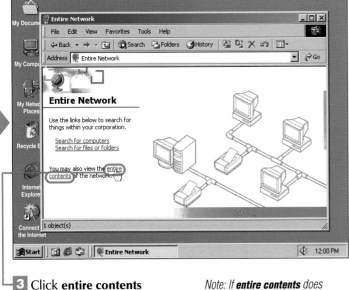

3 Click **entire contents** to continue.

*Note: If **entire contents** does not appear, skip to step 4.*

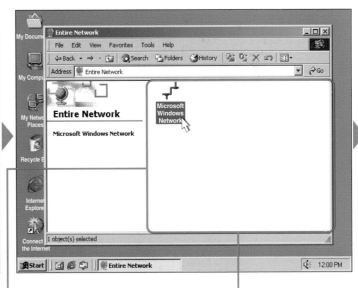

■ The types of networks available appear in this area.

4 Double-click the type of network you want to access.

CONTINUED

You can choose the domain that contains the resources you want to access.

A domain is a collection of computers that are administered together.

BROWSE THROUGH A NETWORK (CONTINUED)

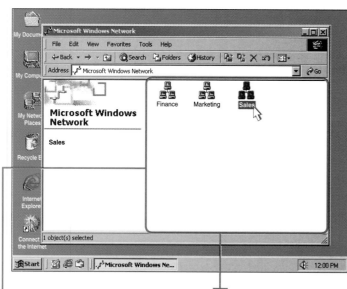

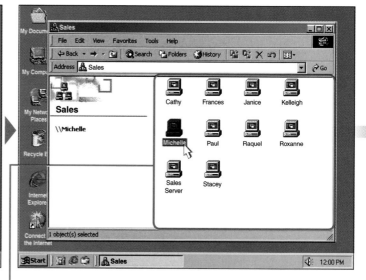

■ This area displays the domains on your network.

5 Double-click the domain containing the computers you want to access.

■ This area displays all the computers in the domain.

6 Double-click the computer containing the files you want to work with.

Note: A dialog box may appear, asking you to enter a user name and password. Contact your system administrator for more information.

TIP

Why does my My Network Places window look different than the window shown below?

The items in your My Network Places window depend on the type of network you use and how the network is set up. There are two main types of networks. A client/server network allows people to store their files on a central computer, called a server. A peer-to-peer network allows people to store and share their files on their own computers.

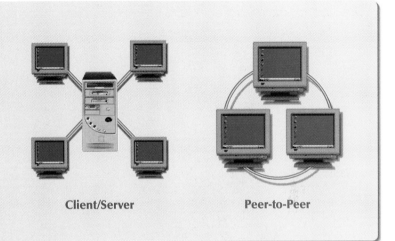

Client/Server　　　**Peer-to-Peer**

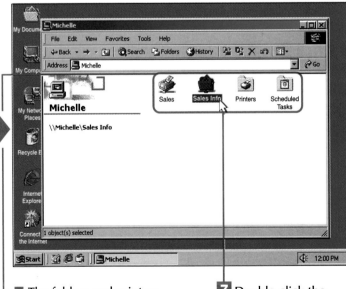

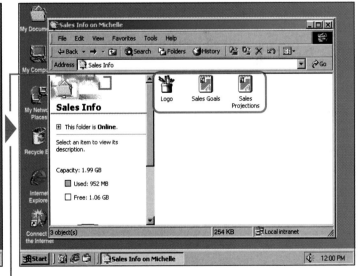

■ The folders and printers shared by the computer appear.

7 Double-click the folder containing the files you want to work with.

■ The contents of the folder appear.

■ You can work with the files and folders as if they were stored on your own computer.

Note: If Windows denies you access to the folder, you do not have permission to access the folder. See page 166 for information on changing permissions for shared folders.

CHAPTER 11

BROWSE THE WEB

Would you like to learn about the World Wide Web? This chapter will show you how to set up an Internet connection and transfer information to your computer from around the world.

The World Wide Web is part of the Internet, which is the largest computer system in the world. The Web consists of a huge collection of documents stored on hundreds of thousands of computers.

WEB PAGES

A Web page is a document on the Web. You can find Web pages on every subject imaginable. There are Web pages that offer information such as newspaper and magazine articles, movie clips, recipes, Shakespearean plays, airline schedules and more. You can also purchase items, do your banking and get programs and games on the Web.

WEB SITES

A Web site is a collection of Web pages maintained by a college, university, government agency, company or individual.

URLS

Each Web page has a unique address, called a Uniform Resource Locator (URL). You can display any Web page if you know its URL.

Most Web page URLs start with http (HyperText Transfer Protocol).

LINKS

Web pages contain highlighted text or images, called links, that connect to other pages on the Web. You can select a link on a Web page to display another page located on the same computer or a computer across the city, country or world.

Links allow you to easily move through a vast amount of information by jumping from one Web page to another. This is known as "browsing the Web."

CONNECTING TO THE INTERNET

Most people use an Internet Service Provider (ISP) to connect to the Internet. Once you pay your service provider to connect to the Internet, you can exchange information on the Internet free of charge.

You can use the Internet Connection wizard to set up your computer to use a connection to the Internet.

Welcome to the Internet

You must be logged on to your computer or network as an administrator to use the Internet Connection wizard. See page 20 to log on to a computer or network.

SET UP A CONNECTION TO THE INTERNET

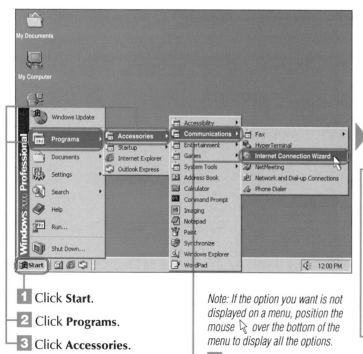

1 Click **Start**.

2 Click **Programs**.

3 Click **Accessories**.

Note: If the option you want is not displayed on a menu, position the mouse over the bottom of the menu to display all the options.

4 Click **Communications**.

5 Click **Internet Connection Wizard**.

■ The Internet Connection wizard appears.

6 To set up your computer to use an existing Internet connection, click this option (○ changes to ⊙).

7 Click **Next** to continue.

Can I set up a connection to the Internet if I do not already have an account with an Internet service provider?

The Internet Connection wizard can help you find an Internet service provider in your area. Perform steps **1** to **6** below, except select **I want to sign up for a new Internet account** in step **6**. Then perform steps **7** to **10**, selecting an Internet service provider you want to use in step **8**.

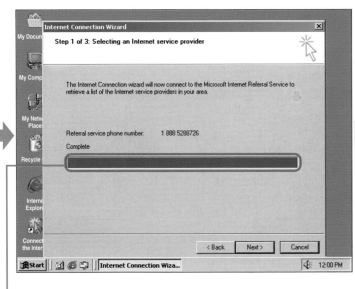

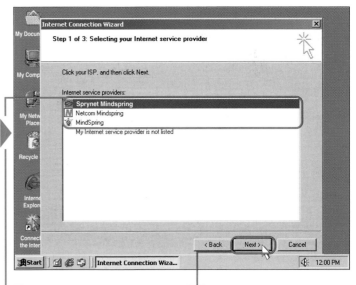

■ The wizard connects to the Microsoft Internet Referral Service to get a list of the Internet service providers available in your area.

■ This area displays the progress of the transfer of information to your computer.

■ When the transfer is complete, a list of Internet service providers in your area appears.

8 Click the name of your Internet service provider.

*Note: If your service provider does not appear in the list, click **My Internet service provider is not listed**.*

9 Click **Next** to continue.

10 Follow the instructions on your screen to finish setting up the computer to use the Internet connection.

You can start Internet Explorer to browse through the information on the Web.

START INTERNET EXPLORER

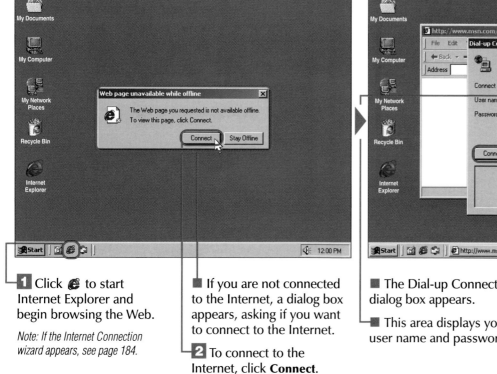

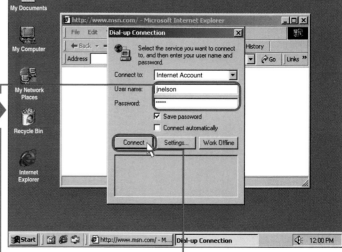

1 Click 🍪 to start Internet Explorer and begin browsing the Web.

Note: If the Internet Connection wizard appears, see page 184.

■ If you are not connected to the Internet, a dialog box appears, asking if you want to connect to the Internet.

2 To connect to the Internet, click **Connect**.

■ The Dial-up Connection dialog box appears.

■ This area displays your user name and password.

Note: A symbol (x) appears for each character in your password to prevent others from viewing the password.

3 Click **Connect** to connect to your Internet service provider.

TIP

Why do the Web pages in this book look different from the Web pages displayed on my screen?

Companies frequently change their Web pages to make the pages more attractive or to add additional information. A Web page displayed on your screen may be a more recent version of the Web page shown in this book.

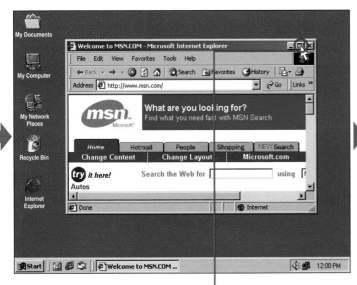

■ The Microsoft Internet Explorer window appears, displaying your home page.

4 Click 🔲 to maximize the window to fill your screen.

■ The window maximizes to fill your screen.

You can easily display a page on the Web that you have heard or read about.

You need to know the address of the Web page you want to view. Each page on the Web has a unique address, called a Uniform Resource Locator (URL).

DISPLAY A SPECIFIC WEB PAGE

1 Click this area to highlight the current Web page address.

2 Type the address of the Web page you want to view and then press the Enter key.

Note: You do not have to type http:// when typing the Web page address.

■ The Web page appears on your screen.

What are some popular Web pages that I can display?

• **Blue Mountain Arts**	www.bluemountain.com
• **CBS SportsLine**	www.sportsline.com
• **CNN**	www.cnn.com
• **eBay**	www.ebay.com
• **maranGraphics**	www.maran.com
• **MSNBC**	www.msnbc.com
• **MTV**	www.mtv.com
• **NASA**	www.nasa.gov
• **Sony**	www.sony.com
• **Time.com**	www.pathfinder.com

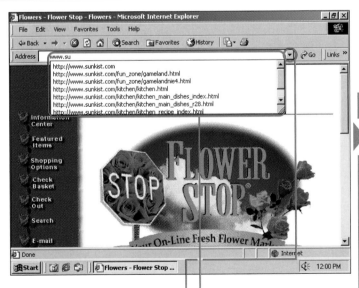

Internet Explorer remembers the addresses of Web pages you recently visited. You can select one of these addresses to quickly redisplay a Web page.

■ When you begin typing the address of a Web page you previously visited, a list of matching addresses appears.

■ You can also click ▾ to display the list of addresses at any time.

1 Click the address of the Web page you want to display.

■ The Web page appears on your screen.

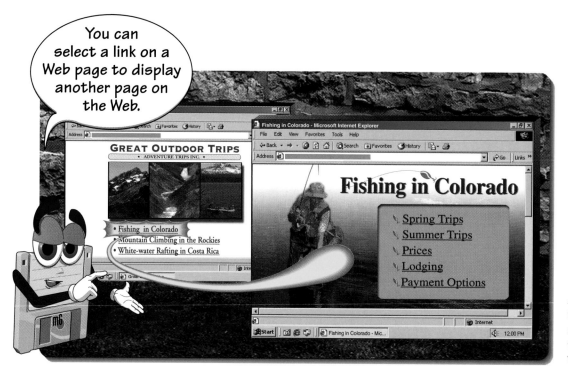

You can select a link on a Web page to display another page on the Web.

A link is highlighted text or an image on a Web page that will take you to another Web page.

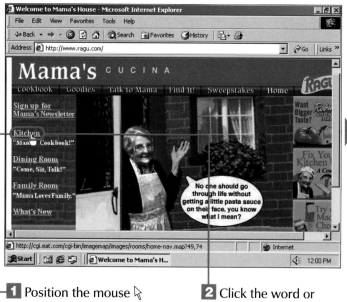

1 Position the mouse ⌖ over a highlighted word or picture of interest. The mouse ⌖ changes to a hand (✎) when over a link.

2 Click the word or picture to display the linked Web page.

■ The linked Web page appears.

■ This area displays the name of the Web page.

■ This icon is animated as the Web page transfers to your computer.

■ This area displays the address of the Web page.

You can easily move back and forth through Web pages you have viewed since you last started Internet Explorer.

MOVE THROUGH WEB PAGES

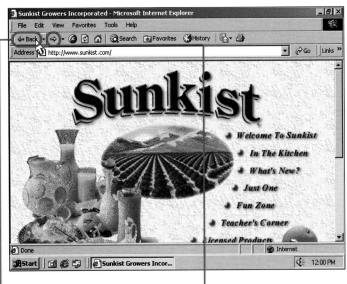

1 Click **Back** to display the last Web page you viewed.

■ Click ➡ to move forward through the Web pages you have viewed.

You can display a list of the Web pages you have viewed.

1 Click ▾ beside **Back** or ➡ to display a list of Web pages you have viewed.

2 Click the Web page you want to view.

You can specify which Web page you want to appear each time you start Internet Explorer. This page is called your home page.

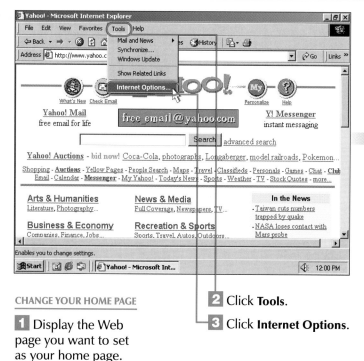

DISPLAY YOUR HOME PAGE

1 Click 🏠 to display your home page.

■ Your home page appears.

Note: Your home page may be different than the home page shown above.

CHANGE YOUR HOME PAGE

1 Display the Web page you want to set as your home page.

2 Click **Tools**.

3 Click **Internet Options**.

Which Web page should I use as my home page?

You can choose any page on the Web as your home page. Your home page can be a Web page you frequently visit or a Web page that provides a good starting point for exploring the Web.

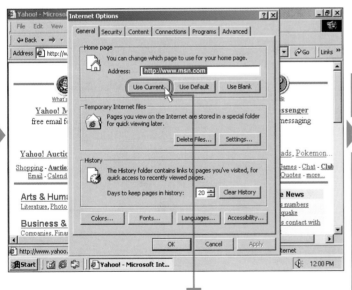

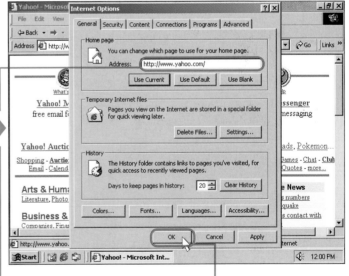

■ The Internet Options dialog box appears.

4 Click **Use Current** to set the Web page displayed on your screen as your new home page.

■ This area displays the address of the new home page.

5 Click **OK** to confirm your change.

You can use the Favorites feature to create a list of Web pages you frequently visit. You can quickly return to any Web page in the list.

ADD A WEB PAGE TO FAVORITES

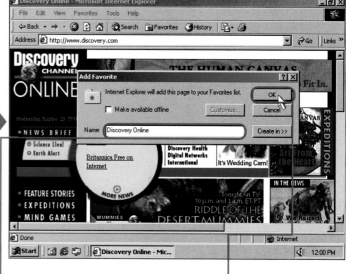

1 Display the Web page you want to add to your collection of favorite Web pages.

2 Click **Favorites**.

3 Click **Add to Favorites**.

■ The Add Favorite dialog box appears.

■ The name of the Web page appears in this area.

4 Click **OK** to add the Web page to your list of favorites.

What are the benefits of adding a Web page to my list of favorites?

Web page addresses can be long and complex. Selecting Web pages from your list of favorites saves you from having to remember and constantly retype the same addresses over and over.

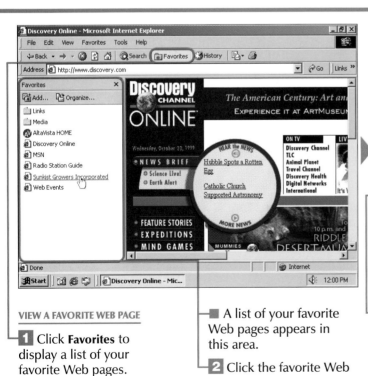

VIEW A FAVORITE WEB PAGE

■1 Click **Favorites** to display a list of your favorite Web pages.

■ A list of your favorite Web pages appears in this area.

■2 Click the favorite Web page you want to view.

Note: To display the favorite Web pages in a folder, click the folder ( ).

■ The favorite Web page you selected appears in this area.

■ You can repeat step 2 to view another favorite Web page.

■3 When you finish viewing your list of favorite Web pages, click **Favorites** to hide the list.

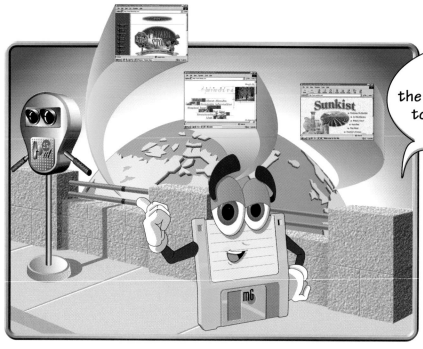

You can find pages on the Web that discuss topics of interest to you.

There are search tools available on the Web that catalog information about millions of Web pages. Popular search tools include Excite, Yahoo! and Lycos.

SEARCH THE WEB

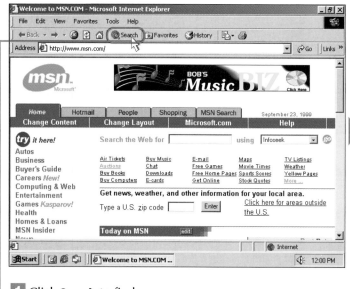

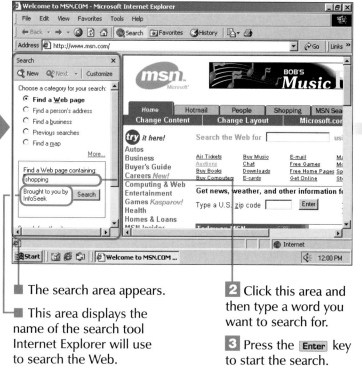

1 Click **Search** to find Web pages of interest.

■ The search area appears.

■ This area displays the name of the search tool Internet Explorer will use to search the Web.

2 Click this area and then type a word you want to search for.

3 Press the Enter key to start the search.

How do search tools find Web pages?

Some search tools use a program, called a robot, to scan the Web for new and updated pages. Thousands of new Web pages are located and cataloged by robots every day. New pages are also cataloged when people submit information about the pages they have created.

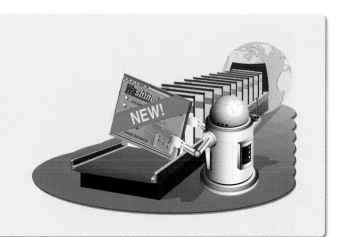

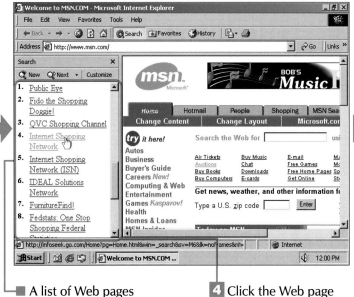

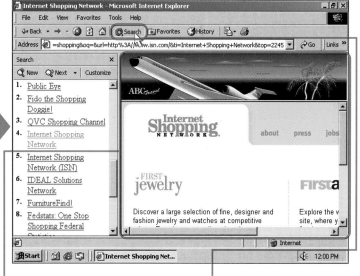

■ A list of Web pages containing the word you specified appears. You may have to use the scroll bar to view the entire list.

4 Click the Web page you want to view.

■ The Web page appears in this area.

5 When you have finished searching, you can click **Search** to hide the search area.

CHAPTER 12

EXCHANGE ELECTRONIC MAIL

Do you want to use your computer to keep in touch with friends and colleagues? Learn how to exchange electronic mail messages in this chapter.

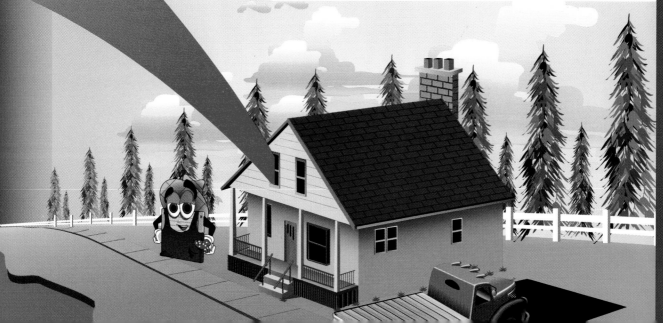

You can start Outlook Express to exchange electronic mail (e-mail) messages with people around the world.

E-mail provides a fast, economical and convenient way to send messages to family, friends and colleagues.

START OUTLOOK EXPRESS

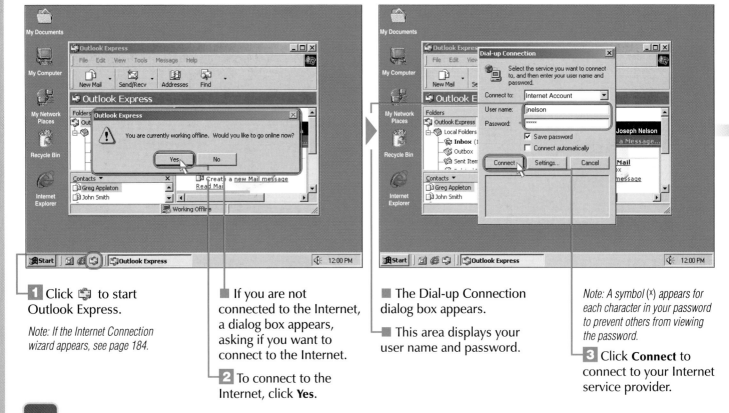

■1 Click 🗐 to start Outlook Express.

Note: If the Internet Connection wizard appears, see page 184.

■ If you are not connected to the Internet, a dialog box appears, asking if you want to connect to the Internet.

■2 To connect to the Internet, click **Yes**.

■ The Dial-up Connection dialog box appears.

■ This area displays your user name and password.

Note: A symbol (ˣ) appears for each character in your password to prevent others from viewing the password.

■3 Click **Connect** to connect to your Internet service provider.

Can I use Outlook Express to e-mail famous people?

You can send a message to anyone around the world if you know the person's e-mail address. Here are the e-mail addresses of some famous people.

NAME	ADDRESS
Bill Gates	askbill@microsoft.com
Brad Pitt	CIAOBOX@MSN.com
James Woods	jameswoods@aol.com
President	president@whitehouse.gov
Tom Brokaw	nightly@nbc.com

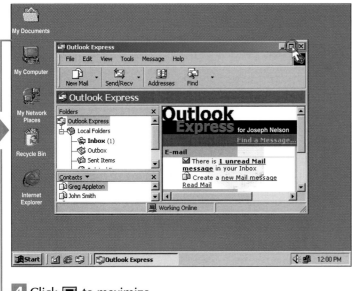

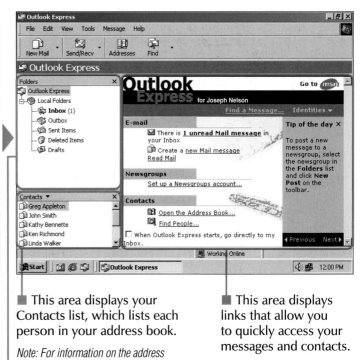

4 Click ▢ to maximize the Outlook Express window to fill your screen.

■ This area displays your Contacts list, which lists each person in your address book.

Note: For information on the address book, see page 206.

■ This area displays the folders that contain your messages.

■ This area displays links that allow you to quickly access your messages and contacts.

You can easily open your messages to read their contents.

Chris,
The drafts for the advertising campaign are ready. Will you be free at 2:00 p.m. tomorrow to discuss them?

- Henry -

READ MESSAGES

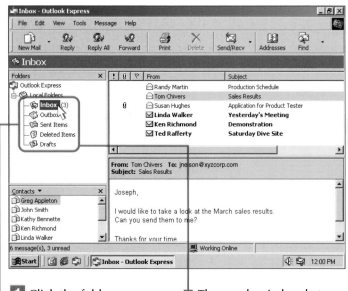

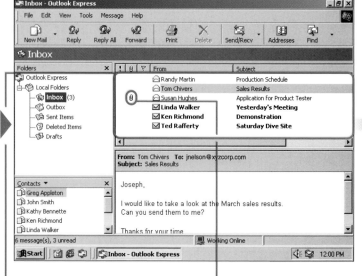

1 Click the folder containing the messages you want to read. The folder is highlighted.

■ The number in brackets beside the folder indicates how many unread messages the folder contains. The number disappears when you have read all the messages in the folder.

■ This area displays the messages in the highlighted folder. Messages you have not read display a closed envelope (✉) and appear in **bold** type.

■ A paper clip icon (📎) appears beside a message with an attached file.

Note: To open an attached file, see page 212.

What folders does Outlook Express use to store my messages?

Inbox

Stores messages sent to you.

Outbox

Temporarily stores messages that have not yet been sent.

Sent Items

Stores copies of messages you have sent.

Deleted Items

Stores messages you have deleted.

Drafts

Stores messages you have not yet completed.

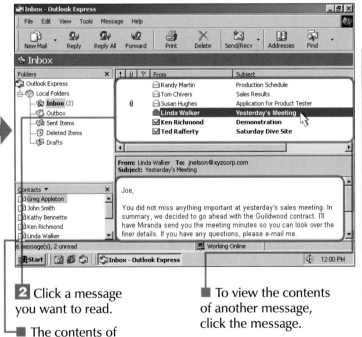

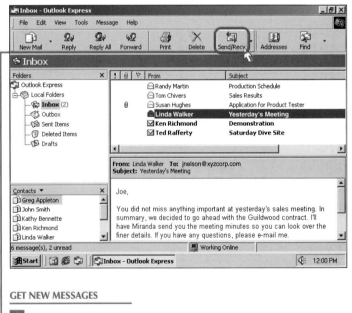

2 Click a message you want to read.

■ The contents of the message appear in this area.

■ To view the contents of another message, click the message.

GET NEW MESSAGES

1 To check for new messages at any time, click **Send/Recv**.

You can send a message to express an idea or request information.

SEND A MESSAGE

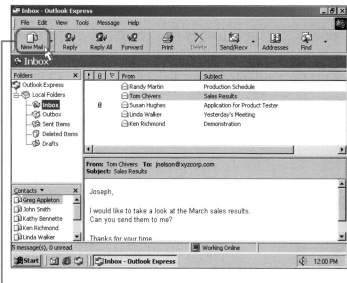

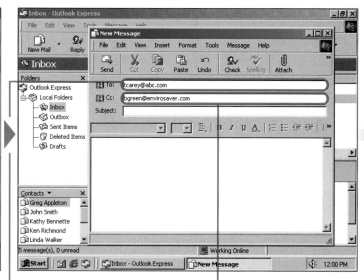

1 Click **New Mail**.

■ The New Message window appears.

2 Type the e-mail address of the person you want to receive the message.

Note: To select a name from the address book, see page 208. Then skip to step 4.

3 To send a copy of the message to a person who is not directly involved but would be interested in the message, click this area and then type the e-mail address.

How can I express emotions in my e-mail messages?

You can use special characters, called smileys or emoticons, to express emotions in e-mail messages. These characters resemble human faces if you turn them sideways.

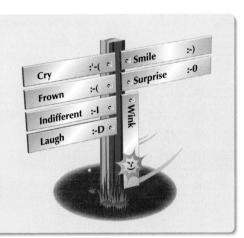

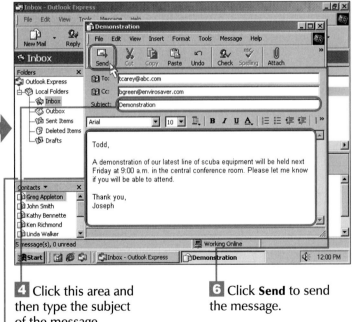

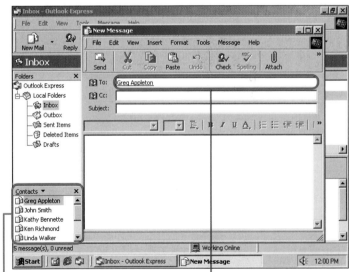

4 Click this area and then type the subject of the message.

5 Click this area and then type the message.

6 Click **Send** to send the message.

■ Outlook Express stores a copy of each message you send in the Sent Items folder.

QUICKLY SEND A MESSAGE

■ The Contacts list displays the name of each person in your address book. For information on the address book, see page 206.

1 To quickly send a message to a person in the Contacts list, double-click the name of the person.

■ The New Message window appears. Outlook Express addresses the message for you.

2 To complete the message, perform steps **3** to **6** starting on page 204.

You can use the address book to store the e-mail addresses of people you frequently send messages to.

ADD A NAME TO THE ADDRESS BOOK

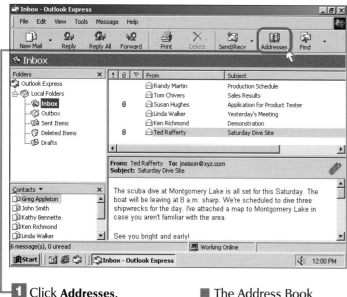

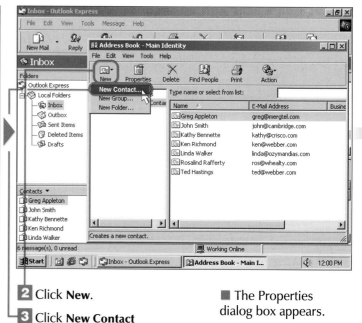

1 Click **Addresses**.

■ The Address Book window appears.

2 Click **New**.

3 Click **New Contact** to add a name to the address book.

■ The Properties dialog box appears.

Can Outlook Express automatically add names to my address book?

Each time you reply to a message, the author's name and e-mail address are automatically added to your address book.

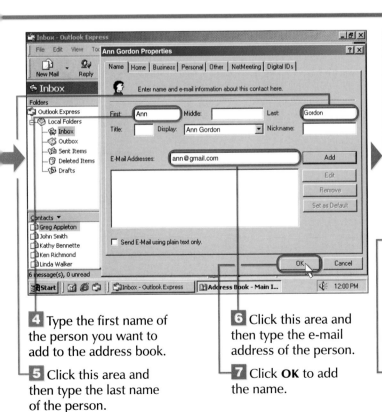

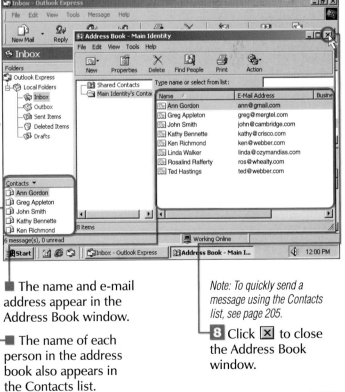

4 Type the first name of the person you want to add to the address book.

5 Click this area and then type the last name of the person.

6 Click this area and then type the e-mail address of the person.

7 Click **OK** to add the name.

■ The name and e-mail address appear in the Address Book window.

■ The name of each person in the address book also appears in the Contacts list.

Note: To quickly send a message using the Contacts list, see page 205.

8 Click ☒ to close the Address Book window.

When sending a message, you can select the name of the person you want to receive the message from the address book.

Selecting names from the address book saves you from having to remember e-mail addresses you often use.

SELECT A NAME FROM THE ADDRESS BOOK

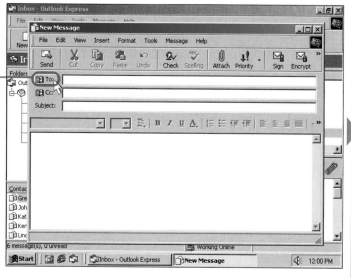

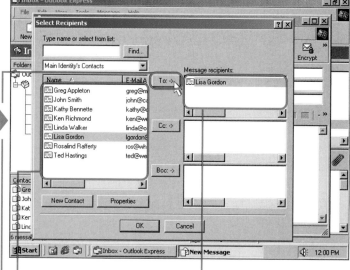

■ To display the New Message window, perform step 1 on page 204.

1 To select a name from the address book, click **To**.

■ The Select Recipients dialog box appears.

2 Click the name of the person you want to receive the message.

3 Click **To**.

■ This area displays the name of the person you selected.

■ You can repeat steps **2** and **3** for each person you want to receive the message.

How can I address a message I want to send?

To

Sends the message to the person you specify.

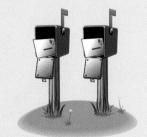

Carbon Copy (Cc)

Sends an exact copy of the message to a person who is not directly involved, but would be interested in the message.

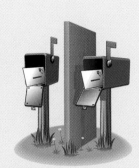

Blind Carbon Copy (Bcc)

Sends an exact copy of the message to a person without anyone else knowing that the person received the message.

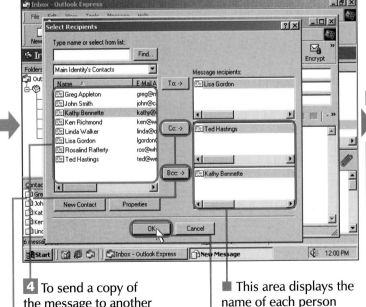

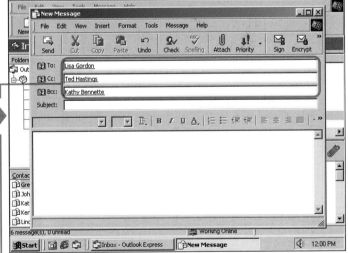

4 To send a copy of the message to another person, click the name of the person.

5 Click **Cc** or **Bcc**.

Note: For more information, see the top of this page.

■ This area displays the name of each person who will receive a copy of the message.

6 Click **OK** to confirm your selections.

■ This area displays the name of each person you selected from the address book.

■ You can now finish composing the message.

You can attach a file to a message you are sending. Attaching a file is useful when you want to include additional information with a message.

ATTACH A FILE TO A MESSAGE

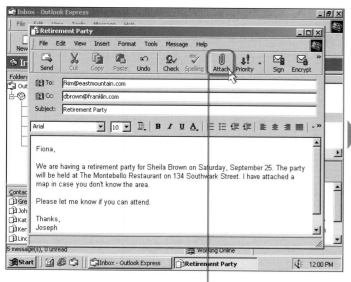

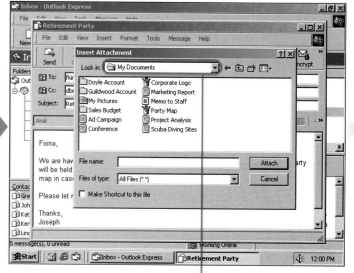

1 To compose a message, perform steps **1** to **5** starting on page 204.

2 Click **Attach** to attach a file to the message.

■ The Insert Attachment dialog box appears.

■ This area shows the location of the displayed files. You can click this area to change the location.

What types of files can I attach to a message?

You can attach files such as documents, pictures, programs, sounds and videos to a message. The computer receiving the message must have the necessary hardware and software to display or play the file.

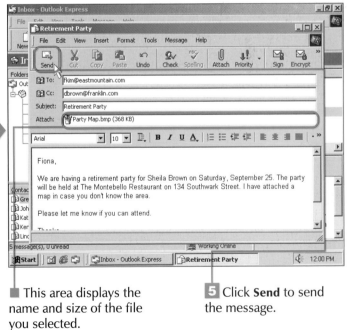

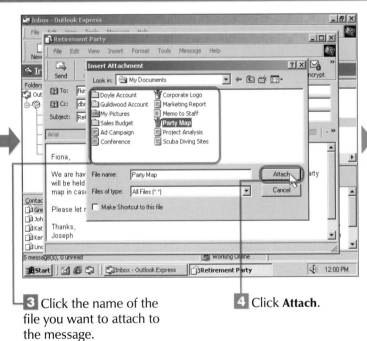

3 Click the name of the file you want to attach to the message.

4 Click **Attach**.

■ This area displays the name and size of the file you selected.

5 Click **Send** to send the message.

VIEW AN ATTACHED FILE

You can view a file attached to a message you receive.

VIEW AN ATTACHED FILE

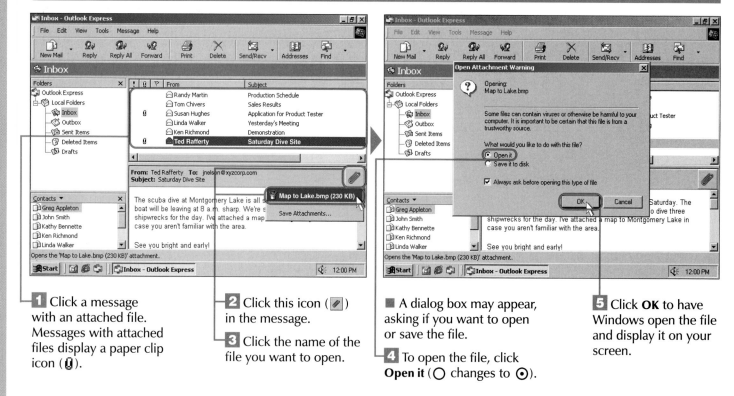

1 Click a message with an attached file. Messages with attached files display a paper clip icon (📎).

2 Click this icon (📎) in the message.

3 Click the name of the file you want to open.

■ A dialog box may appear, asking if you want to open or save the file.

4 To open the file, click **Open it** (○ changes to ⊙).

5 Click **OK** to have Windows open the file and display it on your screen.

212

After reading a message, you can add comments and then forward the message to a friend or colleague.

FORWARD A MESSAGE

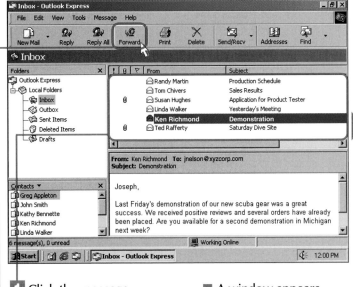

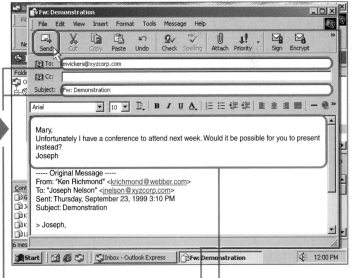

1 Click the message you want to forward.

2 Click **Forward**.

■ A window appears, displaying the message you are forwarding.

3 Type the e-mail address of the person you want to receive the message.

Note: To select a name from the address book, see page 208.

■ Outlook Express fills in the subject for you, starting the subject with **Fw:**.

4 Click this area and then type any comments about the message you are forwarding.

5 Click **Send** to forward the message.

REPLY TO A MESSAGE

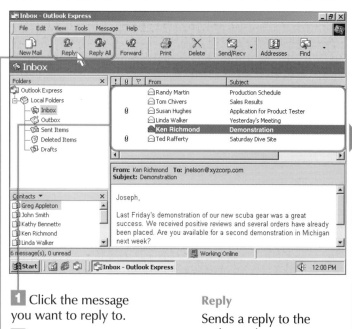

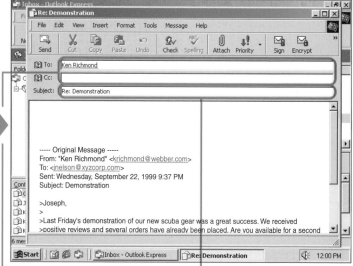

1 Click the message you want to reply to.

2 Click the reply option you want to use.

Reply

Sends a reply to the author only.

Reply All

Sends a reply to the author and everyone who received the original message.

■ A window appears for you to compose the message.

■ Outlook Express fills in the e-mail address(es) for you.

■ Outlook Express also fills in the subject, starting the subject with **Re:**.

How can I save time when typing a message?

Abbreviations are commonly used to save time when typing messages.

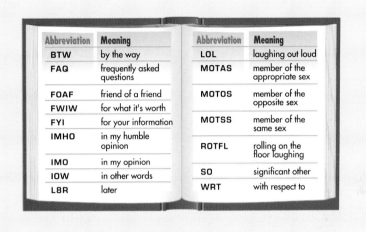

Abbreviation	Meaning	Abbreviation	Meaning
BTW	by the way	LOL	laughing out loud
FAQ	frequently asked questions	MOTAS	member of the appropriate sex
FOAF	friend of a friend	MOTOS	member of the opposite sex
FWIW	for what it's worth		
FYI	for your information	MOTSS	member of the same sex
IMHO	in my humble opinion	ROTFL	rolling on the floor laughing
IMO	in my opinion	SO	significant other
IOW	in other words		
L8R	later	WRT	with respect to

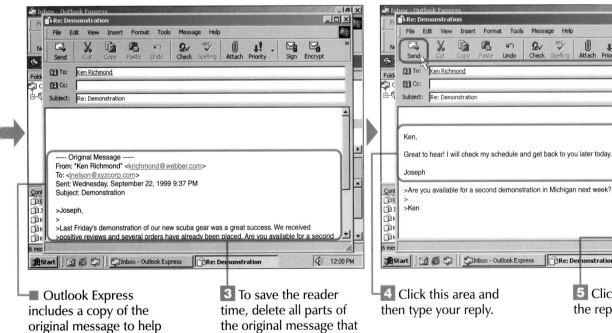

■ Outlook Express includes a copy of the original message to help the reader identify which message you are replying to. This is called quoting.

3 To save the reader time, delete all parts of the original message that do not directly relate to your reply.

4 Click this area and then type your reply.

5 Click **Send** to send the reply.

> You can delete a message you no longer need. Deleting messages prevents your folders from becoming cluttered with messages.

DELETE A MESSAGE

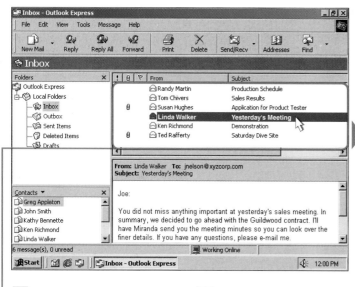

1 Click the message you want to delete.

2 Press the Delete key.

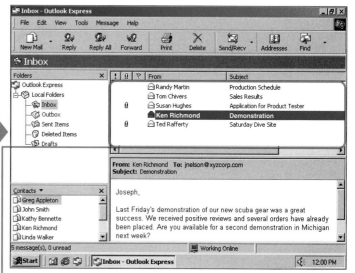

■ Outlook Express removes the message from the current folder and places the message in the Deleted Items folder.

Note: Deleting a message from the Deleted Items folder will permanently remove the message from your computer.

PRINT A MESSAGE

You can produce a paper copy of a message you received.

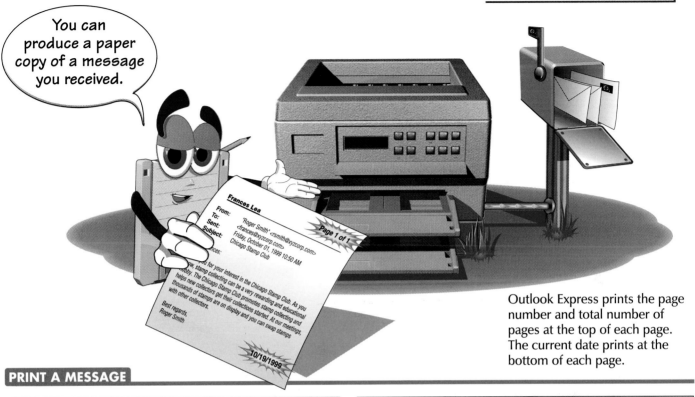

Outlook Express prints the page number and total number of pages at the top of each page. The current date prints at the bottom of each page.

PRINT A MESSAGE

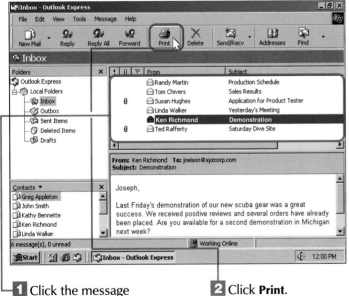

1 Click the message you want to print.

2 Click **Print**.

■ The Print dialog box appears.

■ This area displays the available printers. The printer that will print the message displays a check mark (✔).

3 Click **Print** to print the message.

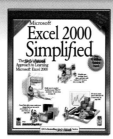

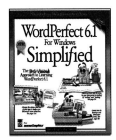

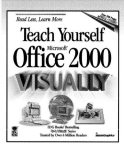

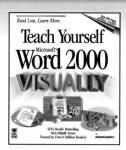

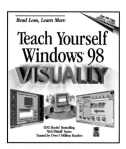

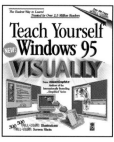

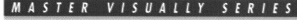

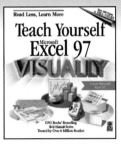

ORDER FORM

IDG BOOKS ®

TRADE & INDIVIDUAL ORDERS

Phone: **(800) 762-2974**
or **(317) 596-5200**
(8 a.m.–6 p.m., CST, weekdays)
FAX : **(800) 550-2747**
or **(317) 596-5692**

EDUCATIONAL ORDERS & DISCOUNTS

Phone: **(800) 434-2086**
(8:30 a.m.–5:00 p.m., CST, weekdays)
FAX : **(317) 596-5499**

CORPORATE ORDERS FOR 3-D VISUAL™ SERIES

Phone: **(800) 469-6616**
(8 a.m.–5 p.m., EST, weekdays)
FAX : **(905) 890-9434**

Qty	ISBN	Title	Price	Total

Shipping & Handling Charges

	Description	First book	Each add'l. book	Total
Domestic	Normal	$4.50	$1.50	$
	Two Day Air	$8.50	$2.50	$
	Overnight	$18.00	$3.00	$
International	Surface	$8.00	$8.00	$
	Airmail	$16.00	$16.00	$
	DHL Air	$17.00	$17.00	$

Subtotal _____

CA residents add
applicable sales tax _____

IN, MA and MD
residents add
5% sales tax _____

IL residents add
6.25% sales tax _____

RI residents add
7% sales tax _____

TX residents add
8.25% sales tax _____

Shipping_____

Total _____

Ship to:

Name_____

Address_____

Company_____

City/State/Zip_____

Daytime Phone_____

Payment: □ Check to IDG Books (US Funds Only)
       □ Visa □ Mastercard □ American Express

Card # _____ Exp. _____ Signature_____

maranGraphics™